I WILL SAY THIS EXACTLY one time

· ESSAYS ·

D. Gilson

SIBLING RIVALRY PRESS
LITTLE ROCK · ARKANSAS

WWW.SIBLINGRIVALRYPRESS.COM

I Will Say This Exactly One Time: Essays
Copyright © 2015 by D. Gilson

Cover design by Seth Pennington

All rights reserved. No part of this book may be reproduced or republished without written consent from the publisher, except by reviewers who may quote brief excerpts in connection with a review in a newspaper, magazine, or electronic publication; nor may any part of this book be reproduced, stored in a retrieval system, or transmitted in any form, or by any means be recorded without written consent of the publisher.

Sibling Rivalry Press, LLC
PO Box 26147
Little Rock, AR 72221

info@siblingrivalrypress.com

www.siblingrivalrypress.com

ISBN: 978-1-937420-99-4

Library of Congress Control Number: 2015948612

First Sibling Rivalry Press Edition, October 2015

For Will,
brother beyond blood

*Your memory is transformative
as opposed to eidetic,
which best served the purposes
of literature or lying.*

- John Keene

ESSAYS

Icarus at Your Local Starbucks: An Introduction	9
Get Rhythm	13
Michael Jackson & Michel Foucault Walk Into a Bar	18
Hey Gurl: Queerness & Romantic Friendship in Poetry	35
The Worst Movie Never Made	48
On Walking	53
Riding in Cars with Brothers	70
Colby Keller for President	74
Britney, Our Lady of Perpetuity	88
On Faggot: An Etymology	92
A Need to Know Basis	102
Essay After Marie Howe	111
Learning to Poem	113
Boys on the Side	119
Dirty Socks: Ke$ha & Queer Theory	125
This Is Not a Suicide Note	132
Elegy for *SkyMall*	138

ICARUS AT YOUR LOCAL STARBUCKS
an introduction to this book

"**WHAT ARE YOU DOING TODAY?**" my father asks during our biweekly talks. I usually call him as I walk to work, an act that provides for a natural and finite end to a conversation in need of parameters. "Headed to work at the coffeeshop," I tell him, which undoubtedly spurns his asking, "You make coffee now?"

I have not been a barista since my freshman year of college, when I did a two-month stint in a small coffeeshop connected to a spa catering to, in the manager's words, "Springfield, Missouri's, Bored Housewives & Fags." I spent the majority of those two months sitting on a crate in the storeroom reading *Vogue* or *US Weekly*, magazines I pilfered from the spa receptionist. This was 2003, so I was obsessed with following the Michael Jackson trial, an obsession for which I am now ashamed, and the utter shit show that was *Bennifer*, the marriage between Jennifer Lopez and Ben Affleck, for which one should never be ashamed. I got fired, and have not worked in coffee ever since, though I do spend copious amounts of time in coffeeshops, a perfectly fitting cliché for the poet / cultural studies scholar I've become / am becoming.

My father does not understand what I "do." Which is not to say he isn't proud; he recently introduced me to a group of men he has coffee with most mornings as, "My youngest child. He's almost a doctor!" But what I do eludes my father.

My father is the middle child, number seven of fourteen, of a poor family from the rocky farmland of central Missouri. His options as an eighteen-year-old boy were clear: work the farm or join the military. My father chose the military, where he trained and worked as a veterinarian. He's great with animals. And with almost any project I've seen him undertake. When my mother and I wanted a bigger house, he built a two-bedroom addition with a bathroom and spacious deck for next to nothing. This is not a skill I have inherited from my father. Though I am confident in my ability to build on the page—and it is an act of building, this art—I do not have his skills to build literal houses, to suture up the wounds of a dog bitten in a rumble at the park, or to change the oil in my car. Which, my father reminds me on almost every one of our biweekly phone calls, I probably haven't done in far too long.

Traditionally masculine fathers—be they soldiers or carpenters or veterinarians or any number of such tactile professions—and their artist sons have long had trouble understanding each other. When Daedalus built the labyrinth, he was locked high in a tower (Rapunzel-style) so his knowledge could be contained. To escape the island of Crete, he built wings for himself and his youngest son, Icarus. Going against his father's warning, Icarus flew too close to the sun, where his wings melted, sending Icarus tumbling to the sea below, where he drowned. It's a lesser-celebrated myth, partially because it goes against American bootstrapism; Icarus flew too high, and it killed him.

Or did it? I want to imagine the myth another way: Icarus didn't drown, but he swam (kind of like Matt

Damon in *Bourne Supremacy*, who swims really far after running his jeep off a tall bridge, a feat that alters the expected trajectory of the film's narrative). Daedalus kept on flying, but Icarus swam. Different paths, strange to the other, perhaps, but paths nonetheless. There's a mythos that many of us become poets because of a broken relationship with our parents; the (over-)worship of Sylvia Plath has encouraged this, no doubt. And maybe I'll never be able to help my father understand what I "do."

But the point of this book is something like that. Here are essays that largely think about what it means to be a poet and cultural theorist in the world. At the most basic level after all, we, the poets and cultural theorists, look at things. Eve Sedgwick explains "that for many of us in childhood the ability to attach intently to a few cultural objects, objects of high or popular culture or both, objects whose meaning seemed mysterious, excessive or oblique in relation to the codes most readily available to us, became a prime resource for survival." Sufjan Stevens sings, "I'm drawn to the blood, / the flight of the one-winged dove. / How? How did this happen?" In these pages I'm stopping to look at people and words and icons, like writers and scholars have always done, though too-often without asking why. Maybe the attempt is in vain / one of vanity, but one I hope we never stop undertaking.

xo, D.

GET RHYTHM

> Sweet is it, sweet is it
> To sleep in the coolness
> Of snug unawareness.
>   - Gwendolyn Brooks

WE ARE DRIVING WEST. We are driving west on Highway 160 between Billings, where my father went to high school, and Aurora, where my mother went to high school, in the maroon Ford Aerostar with the gray stripe. My father is driving and my mother is in the passenger seat beside him and I am behind them, a gray Nintendo Game Boy in my lap. We are driving west and my parents are singing. *When I breeze into that city, people gonna stoop and bow. Ha!* We are driving west and I wish I had remembered my headphones. *All them women gonna make me, teach 'em what they don't know how.* We are driving west although the song is about driving south. *Honey, I'm gonna snowball Jackson.* As we drive, my parents call and respond alongside Johnny and June. As I drive now, some twenty years later on a different highway in a different state, I collapse mythology, imagine my mother as June Carter, my father as Johnny Cash. *Yeah, we're goin' to Jackson, ain't never comin' back.*

We call and we respond not only to the present, but also to a mythos of the past. "Call-and-response patterns," Maggie Sale explains, "provide a basic model that depends and thrives upon audience performance and improvisation, which work together to ensure that the art will be meaningful or functional to the community." Or that it will last. Of course, neither my parents, nor Johnny Cash, nor June Carter, nor the white Christianity they all share invented call and response. We can trace the form back to the Black church in America, and before that to the fields where Black slaves worked, and before that, to Africa, where call and response was a form of democratic communication in civic life. Like so many things, white people have stolen it and rendered it mostly uncool; I think back now to Maranatha, the church camp I attended as a teenager, and the lame camp songs we sang: *Oh you can't get to heaven (oh you can't get to heaven) in a limousine (in a limousine)*. But in my often contradictory opinion, the canon of Cash does a decent enough job with the art form.

Like the song, the poem, too, may be like a call and a response. A myriad pathway between truth, and the world, and perception, and the poet's place within that world. Forgive the pun, but Cash walked the line of truth and perception his entire career. Of his many comeback songs, none holds such a prominent place as "Folsom Prison Blues," where Cash seems to claim he landed himself in prison because, "When I was just a baby my mama told me, *Son, always be a good boy, don't ever play with guns*. But I shot a man in Reno just to watch him die." Like the poet, Cash reveled in this type of myth making, in this art of exaggeration: Johnny spent a night in jail, not prison, just once for carrying methamphetamines into the United States from Mexico without a prescription. He never shot anyone, was not violent in the physical sense, though Cash always tried to live up to his badass perception;

in the 1997 autobiography, he languishes, "I've done no direct physical violence to people, but I certainly hurt many of them." On a recent phone call, my father, currently in chemotherapy and newly taken to talking, to bouts of long, meandering phone conversations, told me something similar, "I've burnt plenty of fields in my life, son."

In the same Ford Aerostar we are driving south. I am a second grader in the front seat next to my father. I am the happiest boy in the world because I am in the front seat next to my father and we are driving south to Disney World. Cash's "The Ballad of Ira Hayes" trickles from the radio, and this is not a happy song, though I don't know it then. *Call him drunken Ira Hayes / He won't answer anymore / Not the whiskey drinkin' Indian / Nor the Marine that went to war.* Listening now, I see how this ballad represents some of Cash's most conflicted feelings of politics and social justice. It is not a happy song and it strikes me that in memory we are not listening to something else, like "Jackson" or maybe "Papa Sang Bass," duets between Cash and Carter, which would become duets between my father and mother as we drove in the Ford Aerostar.

Memory, like the song, like the poem, is conflicted. Why am I in the front seat next to my father? Why is Mom lying down in the back, the very back, of the van, and why is the radio turned low because I remember now my father is saying, "We have to be very quiet. Your mother is upset." It is more than twenty years later, but I call Mom to ask about that trip, if she remembers why we left home so quickly and why she was sleeping in the back. "You don't know?" she asks over the telephone, her voice quiet because my niece is asleep upon her lap. My mother tells me why we went on the trip: her favorite brother, my Uncle Dennis, was dying of AIDS and had called to ask if he could live with us; the next day, my father told my mother he had slept with a woman on a business trip to Kansas City. "I told your father we were getting out of town, taking you to Disney World," my mother tells me now, "I was drugged out of my mind." But in my mind, I am the boy in the front seat next to his father and his mother is just tired but they are going to Disney World so he is the happiest boy in the world. Call this, perhaps, an investment I learned from Johnny Cash: the Sweet Revision of Memory.

Or perhaps it is the Myth of Cash that revises memory, sanitizes memory into art. Or perhaps this revision is the role of the artist, the poet, the songwriter. The biggest hit of Cash's career was 1963's "Ring of Fire," and it is, perhaps more than any other, his signature song. Cash loved classic poetry and in the early sixties, most assumed he wrote the song based on one of his favorite epics, Dante's *Inferno*. But it wasn't Cash who wrote the song, it was his on-again, off-again, poetry-loving mistress, June Carter. Carter wrote the song *about* Cash after finding "Love is like a burning ring of fire" underlined in a book of Elizabethan poetry. Her sister Anita first recorded it, but when Johnny had a dream about falling into a fiery ring as a mariachi band played overhead, he went to June and said he just had to sing the song, and that she, Anita, and their mother Maybelle just had to sing backup. And it seems so funny now: Johnny's biggest hit was penned by the woman with whom he was having an affair, who wrote about how destructive, how damning, loving him could be, and she sang harmony alongside her mother and sister. And it seems so right: that only in the hands of the right person—the artist, the poet, the songwriter—could the lines become immortal.

In Florida, my mother spent most days in the dark bedroom of the condo we rented. Every morning my father said she had a migraine, and we drove off to Disney World, to spinning teacups and Space Mountain. I was the happiest boy in the world then. "But I remember everything," Johnny would sing in his last single, "Hurt," which was actually a cover of Nine Inch Nails. Memory does not always revise so sweetly. Like Cash, the poet must walk a line. Unlike Cash, the poet cannot find it very, very easy to be true.

MICHAEL JACKSON & MICHEL FOUCAULT WALK INTO A BAR

Is it surprising that the cellular prison, with its regular chronologies, forced labor, its authorities of surveillance... should have become the modern instrument of penalty? Is it surprising that prisons resemble factories, schools, barracks, hospitals, which all resemble prisons?

- Michel Foucault, *Discipline & Punish*

That's ignorant.

- Michael Jackson, *Living with Michael Jackson*

A STRING OF SONGS from the late seventies into the mid-eighties aspire to the identity of the American everyman. These are mostly white, working class anthems: John Mellencamp's "Jack & Diane," Journey's "Don't Stop Believin'," Bon Jovi's "Livin' on a Prayer," and especially Bruce Springsteen's "Born in the USA." These are power ballads fallen out of time but not out of favor, sung alike by middle-aged men who were teenagers when the songs first climbed *Billboard* charts, thirty-something women stuck in traffic listening to rush hour radio, and drunken fraternity boys in karaoke bars from Topeka to Tokyo. It would be difficult for me, as it would be for many, I suspect, to say I don't love these songs, though en masse they become a ubiquitous blur, a sprawling shopping center with McDonald's, Wendy's, and Subway, where the chords might be different, but the meat tastes blandly familiar and comforting.

One song from this era also claims universality, but stands astride the crowd: Rockwell's 1984 hit "Somebody's Watching Me." "I'm just an average man," contends the first verse, "with an average life. I work from nine to five; hey hell, I pay the price. All I want is to be left alone in my average home." Rockwell's home was anything but. His given name was Kennedy William Gordy; he was the son of Motown founder Berry Gordy, who claims he named his son after John Kennedy and William "Smokey" Robinson. In 1984 the father and son were estranged, and Rockwell lived with Berry's ex-wife, R&B star Ray Singleton. Somehow, without his father's knowledge, Rockwell attained a recording contract at Motown and wrote his biggest hit about the paranoia of living under the shadow of such a figure. He might have claimed to be average, but he wonders as the first verse moves into the song's bridge, "Why do I always feel like I'm in the Twilight Zone?"

...

The Digital Age has made us all citizens of a surveillance state. How surveyed we are, of course, depends on any number of factors. I live in Washington, DC, one of the most surveyed cities on the planet, and cameras, visible and invisible, watch me as I commute to work, order coffee, go to the gym, and then walk to Captain Cookie & The Milk Man, a food truck with the most delicious vegan chocolate chip cookies I have yet to find. (An iPhone app, MyFitnessPal, estimates this cookie has 250 calories and I will have to run 2.55 miles to burn them off.) If you travel regularly by plane, train, or automobile on our nation's turnpikes and interstates, your picture is taken, your identity checked and cross-checked for general security purposes. Some of this—and my libertarian friends would scoff at me saying this—seems innocent enough, and at times necessary. I've seen enough movies where terrorists take over The White House to know we need their picture, that it helps us not only determine who they are and what they want, but also which rogue agent (Kiefer Sutherland, Harrison Ford, Matt Damon) to send in. God Bless America.

Well, it's easy to say God Bless America as a white guy. If you are a woman, our country is obsessed with surveying your body. In 2012, the state of Virginia passed a law requiring women to get an ultrasound before having an abortion. During early stages of pregnancy, when most abortions are performed, this must be done by penetrating the woman's vagina with a camera. If you appear Latino, you can be asked to prove citizenship at any point, and if you are African American, your body is far less likely to be protected by and three times more likely to be assaulted by our nation's police forces. And god bless you, indeed, if you appear even vaguely Muslim in post-9/11 America.

...

When my father calls to say he has cancer, his first request is "Now I don't want this posted on Facebook." He's mostly concerned two of my sisters, both evangelical Christians, will narrate his battle online, posting a stream of prayer requests as the cancer cells divide and multiply, or praise reports when a doctor tells him his latest blood counts look promising. Our father, a Vietnam veteran, also refuses to call this a "battle" with cancer. He is too rational, and explains scientists are seeing an uptick in lymph node cancers amongst veterans who fought in Southeast Asia and were exposed to Agent Orange. I want to post rabid liberal rants on social media about how the military industrial complex gave my dad cancer. Maybe my father, a scopophobe, should be concerned about his atheist son, too, the one who writes this essay, this act of writing both an agent and conduit of surveillance. What are those burdensome categories of essayistic nonfiction, if not our surveillance of the world, and memoir or confession, if not the surveillance of ourselves?

...

If you begin to search for "Somebody's Watching Me," Google assumes you are looking for Michael Jackson, though it is not his song. Jackson appears on the track as the melodic voice of the chorus—*I always feel like somebody's watching me*. Michael Jackson's fame, of course, eclipsed that of Rockwell, who rests now in relative obscurity. This was especially true in 1984, a year when "Somebody's Watching Me" steadily climbed the *Billboard* charts, yes, but also a year when Jackson ascended his throne, with *Thriller* taking home eight Grammy awards and becoming the best-selling album of all time. The album's title track begins "It's close to midnight and something evil's lurking in the dark." The something remains lyrically vague, though in hindsight this seems a pivotal moment for both Jackson personally and Jackson the cultural zeitgeist. Perhaps the something evil was us, a public that would not stop watching his every move, a gaze Jackson most often welcomed, but a gaze that eventually devoured him. Perhaps the something evil was also Jackson, or rather, his vexed need to be seen and then not seen, a change that would render the adult Jackson confined to his secure homes or various hotel rooms for much of his life. In his 1975 study *Discipline & Punish*, philosopher Michel Foucault argues that not only modern prisons but also schools, hospitals, and the general mechanisms of public society have used the idea of surveillance to make us all self-disciplining citizens. His original French title, in fact, is *Surveiller et Punir*. Jackson, though I cannot claim he read Foucault, seemed keenly aware of the principles therein, and of the irony inherent in the fact that the thing which made him famous eventually also made him a prisoner.

...

"Wherever you go from now on, people will be watching you," Dianna Ross told ten-year-old Michael Jackson in 1968. By 1981, Jackson explained to *Rolling Stone*, "I would sleep on the stage if I could." As the Scarecrow in 1978's *The Wiz*, Michael quoted Henry IV, "Uneasy lies the head that wears a crown," but he wouldn't become known as the King of Pop until 1991, a title he requested for himself in a memo to MTV.

...

In his theory of a modern surveillance society, Foucault put forth the idea that the Panopticon—that circular prison where inmates were constantly watched—is a model for many other systems. He especially distrusted the medical gaze, as outlined in his later book *The Birth of the Clinic,* where the philosopher imagined doctors as co-conspirators with governing régimes, arguing "the struggle against disease must begin with a war against bad government... Man will be totally and definitively cured only if he is first liberated" from eyes who gaze upon him. The symptoms Foucault began exhibiting in the early 1980s would be clear to us now, though biographers, scholars, and activists waver on whether or not Foucault knew he had AIDS.

In a February 2014 interview with the *Telegraph,* the American novelist Edmund White, a friend of Foucault's, claimed that in 1981

> I was warning Foucault about AIDS. When I first told him about the disease he said: "Oh that's perfect Edmund: you American puritans, you're always inventing diseases. And one that singles out blacks, drug users and gays – how perfect!"... I tried to insist that it was real despite its ideological aspects... The doctors were intimidated by Foucault's anti-medicine stance. They didn't want to be accused of having a paternalistic or an I'm-better-than-you attitude. He himself wasn't sure what his illness was until the last few months.

I find it hard to believe Foucault was so ingrained in his own ideology that he didn't know he had AIDS until the very end. He lived in Paris, after all, spending a majority of his time outside France in either San Francisco or New York, epicenters of gay men's health. While in residence at Berkeley during the seventies, he was a frequent visitor to Bay Area bathhouses. How could he not know? But this is easy for me to say as a gay man in the twenty-first century. And in examining Foucault's past, I aim not to shame but to understand: he, like many of us, didn't want his body to be under the surveillance of anyone, let along prodding doctors at a moment when many thought those with AIDS had only themselves to blame. Perhaps he chose not to know, one of the few choices we are truly offered.

...

As a teenager I was diagnosed with hypochondria, so my need to know has long trumped any desire to remain blissfully unaware. At sixteen, I let a businessman jack me off in the steam room of the Pat Jones YMCA in Springfield, Missouri; I immediately left the gym and stopped at Walgreen's, purchasing an $89 HIV-home-testing kit, which I performed in the bathroom of a library and dropped in the mail to await my phone-in test results. Of course this was ignorant, both of how HIV is spread and its incubation period, but when it comes to issues of the body, I have always assumed the worst. So when I returned from Washington to Missouri one weekend this past June to visit my parents, and my father complained of a swell on the right side of his neck, I quickly asked, "Could it be a tumor?" *No*, said my father and mother, both of whom worked in medicine before retiring; it was just summer allergies or a cold. When one, then two, then three rounds of antibiotics didn't relieve the swelling, my father's doctor ordered a biopsy. By mid-August, Dad called to tell me had cancer.

Of course, sometimes, the complicated decision to

know renders us suspended in life, if not entirely saved. In an exploratory surgery, my father's doctors found a cluster of small tumors in his throat and nasal cavities. The prognosis was good, albeit complicated: the growths were lymphoma, an easily treatable cancer, but one my father would live with for the rest of his life. For the rest of his life, my father will have quarterly positron emission tomography (PET) scans, where a radioactive tracer will course through his body and make diseases glow neon green or electric blue on a laboratory computer screen. I ask Dad, who hates to be photographed or discussed or dwelt upon, if this bothers him. "What are you going to do?" he answers, shrugging his shoulders.

A similar philosophical quandary rocked Michael Jackson since his late teens, though under different circumstances altogether. Diagnosed in 1983 with vitiligo, a disease that causes areas of the epidermis to lose pigmentation, Jackson began treatments—not to appear whiter because he was ashamed of being black, but to even out his increasingly blotchy complexion, an understandable vanity given the public circulation of Jackson's image. He was, Jackson regularly claimed, first and foremost a dancer, destined to be gazed upon. Thus began the complicated relationship Jackson would have with the medical community until well after his death.

...

During the filming of a Pepsi commercial in January of 1984, Jackson's hair caught fire, causing second- and third-degree burns. In 1993, Jackson would admit this was when he started taking painkillers, an addiction for which his friends Elizabeth Taylor and Elton John finally convinced Jackson to enter rehab, though his sober days following treatment would be few and far between, according to sources from Janet Jackson to Michael Bashir. Prescription drug overdose—Propofol and Benzodiazepine particularly—eventually led to cardiac arrest and Jackson's death in the summer of 2009. Yet the medical gaze that so consumed public discussions of Jackson were those of his plastic surgeries: rhinoplasty, chin cleft, cheekbone reconstruction, lip alteration (to give but a few of the speculations). What consumed us most fervently, however, was Jackson's ever-changing nose, reconstructed initially to resemble that of Bobby Driscoll, the child actor who served as the voice for Walt Disney's 1953 *Peter Pan*. Though a metaphoric trifecta between Foucault, my father, and Jackson seems implausible, admittedly impossible, it bothers me now, when I see how my father hates not only the gaze of his doctors but also the pitying looks of his wife and children, that we all treated Jackson so obsessively—obsessing, as his doctors, well-meaning or not, must have obsessed, over the star's ever-changing look, an obsession we justified in the name of concern for our icon. Perhaps it was escape that drove Jackson to wear disguises, to surgically alter his appearance. As he prophesied in 1987's "Price of Fame": "I want a face no one can recognize."

...

Scopophobia, sometimes called ophthalmophobia, is the fear of being stared at. In the age of social media, it would seem few suffer from this condition. We snap selfies, pictures of the food we are eating, the coffee we are drinking, the friends we are hanging out with, and approaching thunderstorms from the patios of our parents' homes, as I have just done while sitting with my father the afternoon before his first exploratory surgery. We upload these to Facebook or Twitter or Tumblr or Instagram or Pinterest. We write clever captions punctuated by hashtags, "New shirt for new job! #Successories" or "Not to be one of *those* people but LOOK at this macaroni & cheese! #FoodPorn." We live in a world of exclamation points, when our daily lives are usually a series of commas, ellipses, periods, and semi-colons. A wise writing professor I had for the course "Modern Grammars" told us, "If you're lucky, you get one, maybe two exclamation points a year."

I am guilty of this, too. I have announced publications and promotions on Facebook, ranted about long lines at Starbucks on Twitter, Tumbled pictures of assholes who double-park their BMWs at my local Whole Foods. What am I saying? I am an asshole. What is perhaps more frightening: people have liked these, shared these, retweeted them. I can log on at any point in the day and know exactly what my friends are doing, what they're reading, where they're eating, and how they feel about this unseasonably cool September day. What is perhaps more puzzling is that at any point I can log on and know what people I would not even consider friends are doing: that guy from elementary school who moved to Japan, an old co-worker from The Gap who is now a Jehovah's Witness, or my second cousin in Iraq. I've met him once. And what is he doing? Playing Halo and drinking contraband whiskey outside Fallujah. He reports, "This is fucking awesome, dudes!"

...

Obese and twelve years old, I told a therapist my biggest fear was my father watching me eat. I was not really afraid of this, though it annoyed me when we were at McDonald's and Dad would watch me squirt a big glob of ketchup on a napkin, stir in salt, and dip greasy French fries from tabletop to mouth. Obviously, this was a deflection: I was afraid of being abandoned but didn't want to talk about it. Years later, I would relate this story to a different therapist in a different state. He would tell me this wasn't deflection, but my unconscious surfacing: "Classic Oedipal complex. Your biggest fear is your father catching you with a penis in your mouth."

...

When Michael Jackson was accused of molesting Jordan Chandler in 1993, Santa Barbara County sheriff's officers were issued a warrant to photograph and video Jackson's entire naked self, "including his penis, anus, hips, buttocks and any other part of his body." Allegedly, the thirteen-year-old Chandler had described to police white blotches on Jackson's genitalia in detail, which incensed the public even more, many of whom thought Jackson was not only a child molester but also attempting to become white before our very eyes. In reality, Jackson bleached his skin because of vitiligo. But the police demanded to examine the most intimate parts of Jackson's body, a surveillance that left us, his public, tantalized.

...

In line for security at Chicago's O'Hare International, one of the busiest airports in the world, I found myself approaching a sexy TSA agent. I do not particularly have a uniform fetish, but suffice it to say, he filled out his baby blue shirt and navy slacks quite nicely; about thirty-five, he wore his facial hair long enough to accentuate but not hide his Roman jaw; his eyes were bright green. I took out my phone in attempt to snap a picture of him, which I would send to a friend with the caption: "Can I request a TSA strip search, or is that against protocol?" Suddenly, the man behind me tapped my shoulder and asked what I was doing. "Um, taking a picture of the hot guy," I told him as he removed a badge from his jacket pocket. He was a United States Air Marshall.

In an interview room off the B Terminal, I learned Homeland Security is highly suspicious of people taking covert pictures of federal officers. The marshals went through my luggage and asked a series of questions. *Where are you going?* Missouri. My dad has cancer. *How long will you be there?* Three days if his surgery goes well. *You're flying in from Washington?* Yes. I'm a PhD student there. *In what?* English. *Why were you taking a picture of a federal officer in a busy airport?* Because he was hot.

...

The German literary critic Walter Benjamin explains, "The scene of a crime, too, is deserted, it is photographed for the purpose of establishing evidence." If you Google "how often are we photographed," as I have just done, the first search result is from a forum at What to Expect®, an online community on pregnancy and parenting. The question prompting the forum comes from a woman named Sharon, who asks, "How often should we have professional baby photos taken?" I have known parents who do this monthly, though in many multi-child households I have noticed the frequency of pictures decreases with subsequent children. My sister Jennifer, for instance, had photos taken incessantly of her first child, my niece Natalie. Natalie's sister Nicole, born seventeen months later, was photographed decidedly less. Their third, my nephew Nicholas, has few baby photos. My sister expresses regret over this, as I have heard other parents do. Perhaps they know Benjamin is right, that our lives are all crime scenes in a sense, and happy baby photos relieve parents from blame. "See," they can tell their adult children, "you were happy once and here is proof."

...

Michael Jackson fascinates us so much, I believe, because he simultaneously fulfills our biggest fantasies and our biggest fears. A poor kid from Gary, Indiana, Jackson worked hard—harder than most of us ever work—from the age of four to overcome poverty. He was the American Dream anew: rich and known by everybody, but yet nobody. Not surprisingly, though shamefully, Jackson frightens us because he both transcends and overflows our knowable markers of race, gender, and sexuality. In her book *Dangerous*, Susan Fast explains, "The overarching thematic in Jackson's art and life is what has often been viewed as his 'transgression' of normative boundaries." For over four decades we surveyed him—*Is Jackson black or white? Does he want to be a woman? He's gay, right?*—but even after his death in the summer of

2009, we've found few answers.

My siblings are much older, born in the late sixties and early seventies; they grew up alongside Jackson, and because I worshiped them as a young child, some of my earliest memories are dancing to "Thriller" or "Smooth Criminal" with my sister Jennifer and her friends. I vaguely remember the early nineties child molestation scandal, though solely through the lens of my parents' comments as we sat watching nightly news from our living room in the Ozarks. My first knowing surveillance of Jackson came on September 8, 1994. Michael Jackson opened the tenth anniversary of the MTV Video Music Awards by bringing his new bride, Lisa Marie Presley, the daughter of Elvis, onstage. "Welcome to the MTV Video Music Awards," Jackson greeted audiences with a sly smile, Lisa Marie at his side, unsure of what to do with her hands. "I'm very happy to be here," he continued, "And just think, everybody thought this wouldn't last." Jackson smiled, pulled the Ray-Ban Aviators off his face, and kissed Lisa Marie.

What I remember then, a memory confirmed now by watching clips of the kiss online, was how forced it all seemed. How Jackson appeared to be trying to prove something. How Presley took part, but quickly pulled away from the kiss and subtly pushed her husband away.

...

I am not a scopophobe. I like to be watched. In bars men with husbands pull me into the bathroom and stick their tongues into my mouth because we both know we are being watched, or that we might get caught, and that there is something at stake here. But I like how they begin to watch my body on the dance floor, hungry, how I can catch their gaze and return it. I do this one night with a colleague, David, and stupidly he texts me to say, "Kissing you is like calamine lotion to my seven-year-itch." His partner of seven years, Steven, finds the text on David's phone, left on their kitchen counter as David takes their dogs out to piss.

...

In June of 2013, the Obama administration admitted to a broad-reaching surveillance program in which it tapped the phone lines and scoured the communications records of tens of millions of Americans and foreigners alike. The probe went as far as the cellphone of Germany's Prime Minister Angela Merkel, despite the fact that her government is one of the United States' biggest allies. People were rightfully pissed and in response the Obama White House released a white paper defending as both constitutional and reasonable this continuation of Bush-era politicking that stole civil liberties in a vague, ongoing, all-encompassing War on Terror. The white paper claims Justice Department officials need only find a person's "relevance" to terror, easy in post-9/11 America, and that relevance is "a broad standard that permits discovery of large volumes of data in circumstances where doing so is necessary to identify much smaller amounts of information within that data that directly bears on the matter being investigated." If, as pundits and scholars have argued, it was the significant millennial vote that ushered Obama into office under vague promises of hope and change, it is clear now that little had changed from administrations prior. What is less clear, though plausible, is that millennials welcome surveillance into their lives.

...

"Scream," Jackson's 1995 duet with his sister Janet and the lead single from his ninth album *HIStory*, is an anthem against surveillance in many ways. Here are two stars we've watched neurotically since early childhood, the most successful members of a, let's be honest, fucked up family. Michael, fresh off a settlement for child abuse allegations in 1993, aimed the song at American media: "Stop pressurin' me. Just stop pressurin' me. Stop fuckin' with me," the chorus rings. But the blame is complicated. Certainly the media obsessed over Michael, has always obsessed over him and continues to even in death, but they wouldn't if we ourselves didn't demand the obsession. Further, Jackson himself is not blameless; he lived a lifestyle that required such infamy. He even fed sensational stories to the tabloids himself before the molestation charges completely changed the public tenor. By all accounts, Jackson's desire for attention and adoration was insatiable, which leaves us in both awe and fear, for him and for ourselves.

...

The TSA urges us all: *If You See Something, Say Something*. The phrase, trademarked by the US Department of Homeland Security, can be heard over the loudspeakers of our airports and on posters adorning transit systems across the country. I ride the Washington Metro and see them every day. One especially telling poster explains that now I can text in the suspicious behavior I see. It is a strange thing, this desire to be safe, to act accordingly, and yet to be seen. It is a struggle for power against both ourselves and those we elect to watch us. It is not unlike what Foucault saw in the past and predicted for the future in *Discipline & Punish*.

The effect of the prison system, which mirrors the general shift of a culture that assumes we are always watched and watching, is that we are now self-governing. Foucault describes the public prisoner: "He who is subjected to a field of visibility, and who knows it, assumes responsibility for the constraints of power; he makes them play spontaneously upon himself; he inscribed in himself the power relation in which he simultaneously plays both roles; he becomes the principle of his own subjection." In the digital age, our self-governing becomes public spectacle as we willfully give over our private lives not only to an online community of friends, but also the police, the IRS, the military, the banks... Our own willingness to give up our lives as art objects becomes a right to demand such transparency from others, from our friends and coworkers, from our politicians and celebrities.

...

Following the death of Michael Jackson, Pew Research found two-thirds of Americans thought media coverage of the star was excessive, and yet eighty percent of Americans polled also said they followed the coverage enthusiastically.

HEY GURL:
QUEERNESS & ROMANTIC FRIENDSHIP
IN POETRY

IT IS WINTER, THE COLDEST, snowiest one Washington has had in years. I don't like this town, its general stuffiness, though I love school, as I always have. Last year I assisted a professor who grew up in the same suburban DC neighborhood as Eve Sedgwick; I dated a man whose dissertation was chaired by the late theorist; for a week on my way to and from school, I read and re-read her essay "White Glasses" on a crowded Metro bus. In writing on her friendship with the poet Michael Lynch, Sedgwick wonders, "If what is at work here is an identification that falls across gender, it falls no less across sexualities, across 'perversions.' And across the ontological crack between the living and the dead." So as I read this, I'm thinking of how I came to be queer and now, about the boundaries between what is a poet and what is a scholar, about the boundaries between friendship and romance and eroticism, and about the relationship we have with both the literature and theory we read.

In the winter of 1952, Frank O'Hara took the advice of his psychiatrist, cutting the co-dependent ties he had with an alcoholic he loved dearly. "Save yourself," the doctor told the poet and museum curator, "You can't do anything about your mother." O'Hara had traveled home from his beloved New York to Grafton, Massachusetts, explaining this need for independence to the matriarch of the O'Hara clan. In the circle of New York School painters O'Hara considered his closest friends, one woman, Grace Hartigan, stood on the periphery, though she had always intrigued the poet. Later that winter, the two friends would become the closest of intimates; it is their budding relationship—one of romantic friendship, assuredly—and the art that results from it that I cannot stop thinking about.

Upon O'Hara's prodigal return to New York City at the end of February, biographer Brad Gooch explains the upward momentum of O'Hara and Hartigan's relationship well:

> When O'Hara returned to New York, his friendship with the painter Grace Hartigan began to intensify. O'Hara was, in fact, very upset by the break with his mother, and Hartigan, who had never felt his mother was exactly a good influence, tried to comfort him during this crucial time. "I never met Frank's mother," says Hartigan. "I didn't want to because I was so loyal to Frank and I thought she caused him so much pain." Hartigan was going through a transition of her own—one of many. She had a son from a first marriage in Elizabeth, New Jersey. She then briefly married ex-Marine and painter Harry Jackson, though their marriage was annulled soon after a honeymoon in Mexico.

The poet and the painter came together in a tumultuous time in their individual lives, out of crisis and into a sort of queer collectivity, I posit in the vein of José Muñoz, that allowed for their artistic collaborations, a type of utopia reaching, to flourish. Though this collaborative aspect of their friendship is essential historically, and well documented critically in projects like Marjorie Perloff's *Frank O'Hara: Poet Among Painters*, what I am most interested in here is their romantic friendship as expressed through the little poem "For Grace, After a Party," and further, how that friendship is, at least potentially, one of great queerness.

But before I turn to that intimacy, it seems important here to briefly consider a historicity of intimacy in the short form poem. In a strange stream of connection, akin to an echo that Lynne Huffer senses when she "meets" Foucault in the archive of both her life and research, Frank O'Hara's poetic harkens back to Shakespeare's. It was Shakespeare, after all, who gives us the earliest model of a sequence of poems between two people: his *Sonnets*, the first 126 written to a young man and the remainder, with some breakage, written to the racially Othered "dark lady." Over four hundred years later in his 1959 manifesto, O'Hara founds a new—oh, but it isn't new—literary movement, proclaiming:

> Personism, a movement which I recently founded and which nobody knows about, interests me a great deal, being totally opposed to this kind of abstract removal that it is verging on a true abstraction for the first time, really, in the history of poetry... Personism has nothing to do with philosophy, it's all art... But to give you a vague idea, one of its minimal aspects is to address itself to one person (other than the poet himself), thus evoking overtones of love without destroying love's life-giving vulgarity, and sustaining the poet's feelings towards the poem while preventing love from distracting him into feeling about the person.

What opens up here is, perhaps, a queer space of desire-triangulation between the poet, the poem, and the addressee[1]. O'Hara quickly moves to praising his ideal, explaining Personism is "a very exciting movement which will undoubtedly have lots of adherents. It puts the poem squarely between the poet and the person, Lucky Pierre style, and the poem is correspondingly gratified. The poem is at last between two persons instead of two pages." Perhaps the poem can open upon a queerness the Renaissance scholar Will Stockton demands be tied to the body's "antiheteronormative modes of embodiment," while also opening up the literal and literary queer space of the poem itself.

Further, the queer space evoked here necessitates queer, as opposed to straight, time. O'Hara, not surprisingly, was just rearticulating an idea we know already exists with Shakespeare—that the poem can be between two persons—and conceivably even earlier[2]. In his book *Cruising Utopia*, where O'Hara is a central figure of study, José Muñoz places the importance of a potentially queer time in sync with literary and cultural analysis—

> I begin this chapter on futurity and a desire that is utopian by turning to a text from the past—more specifically, to those words that emanate from the spatiotemporal coordinate Bloch referred to as the no-longer-conscious, a term that attempts to enact a

---

1 In fact, it is often said of O'Hara's work that the poems could easily have just been letters, postcards, or phone calls made from the poet to his friends, lovers, and intimates.

2 Or in the very least, I hope earlier, from the beginning of poetry. I never want to give Shakespeare the credit for having invented the human and thus the world, as some scholars have been apt to do.

more precise understanding of the work that the past does, what can be understood as the performative force of the past.

O'Hara the poet, thus, does not exist without Shakespeare the poet, and I, a poet-scholar, without both of them. Nor does Shakespeare hold literary and cultural meaning without both O'Hara and I writing in a queer time that follows the Bard's own present into a future which is now the past *and* a future which is always yet to come. As such, queerness is both completely historical and ahistorical, a both-and-ness possible only, I am beginning to think, through the meaning making of a capacious queerness that does not leave behind the bodies of real-life living homos, in the case of O'Hara and I, to borrow a term from Kevin Floyd, or the always-haunting Shakespeare, whichever being of sexuality we wish to assign him[3].

Queer time necessitates that we join a dual-lineage of both historicity and futurity. Thank god that the poem—and the larger project of the poem, the poetic—is between two people at last. Indeed, my own work, I humbly offer, enters an intimacy with both Shakespeare, through the sonnet form found throughout my poetry, and O'Hara, through both the textual experience of learning to read by reading him as a child and the energy that I hope, in even some fractious way, continues from his lines into my own. Muñoz beautifully mines O'Hara's widely anthologized "Having a Coke with You" for not

---

3 See also the litany of scholars working to "queer" a Shakespeare that existed way before any modern sense of queerness as sexuality. Menon's (problematic, to euphemize best I can) introduction to the collection *Shakesqueer* (Duke UP, 2012) is but one prominent example.

only the utopian possibilities, but also the intimacy, the between-personesses, that verse contains. "Having a Coke with You," Muñoz contends,

> tells us of a quotidian act, having a Coke with somebody, that signifies a vast lifeworld of queer relationality, an encrypted sociality, and a utopian potentiality. The quotidian act of sharing a Coke, consuming a common commodity with a beloved with whom one shares secret smiles, trumps fantastic moments in the history of art. Though the poem is clearly about the present, it is a present that is now squarely the past and in its queer relationality promises a future. The fun of having a Coke is a mode of exhilaration in which one views a restructured sociality.

The exhilarated queer intimacy is evident in O'Hara's poetic, and especially so in a poem like "Having a Coke with You," where the utopian future of a very gay relationship between two men, one infused with both sexual and aesthetic concerns, is, seemingly, only a page away. But so many of O'Hara's most intimate poems are positioned between the poet and women, celebrities, such as Billie Holiday or Lana Turner, or close friends, such as Bunny Lang or Grace Hartigan, the latter of whom is especially intriguing to me now, at a time in my own life where I cannot shake the romantic friendships I have been having with women all along.

A few years into their budding romance—I do not know what else to call it—O'Hara writes this little poem to Grace Hartigan:

For Grace, After a Party

    You do not always know what I am feeling.
Last night in the warm spring air while I was
blazing my tirade against someone who doesn't
interest
    me, it was love for you that set me
afire,
    and isn't it odd? for in rooms full of
strangers my most tender feelings
                        writhe and
bear the fruit of screaming. Put out your hand,
isn't there
    an ashtray, suddenly, there? beside
the bed? And someone you love enters the room
and says wouldn't
            you like the eggs a little
different today?
        And when they arrive they are
just plain scrambled eggs and the warm weather
is holding.

    Muñoz poignantly speaks to the queer relationality (and utopia) of a poem like "Having a Coke with You," but I'm curious now, what is that queer relationality when the poet turns to writing about how his "most tender feelings / writhe and / bear the fruit of screaming" not for a male body, the expected object(s) of his sexual desire, but for a female friend, one with whom he often quarreled as a lover might quarrel, with whom he often collaborated, traveled, and for whom he confessed a romantic love?
    To put it simply: what happens when a gay man

has a crush on a woman? The poem itself admits the feelings from (homosexual) O'Hara to (heterosexual) Hartigan[4] are quite surprising; perhaps this is especially so considering O'Hara's better known poems like "Having a Coke with You," which are markedly homosexual in their desiring. Yet, O'Hara is not satisfied to live in the completely static, dystopic terrain of the homo-hetero binary and begins by dispelling what is expected of him and his desire: "You do not always know what I am feeling." If "Having a Coke with You" brings homosexual desiring to the quotidian, surely "For Grace, After a Party," queers the quotidian between a homo- and heterosexual. This quotidian nature is evident when O'Hara, speaking about Hartigan, explains how "someone you love enters the room / and says wouldn't / you like the eggs a little / different today?" but they end up being "just plain scrambled eggs." Gooch points to this everydayness of their relationship, explaining O'Hara "and Hartigan became pals—often talking on the phone about parties, art, boyfriends. They shared an enthusiasm for movies, as well as for fanzines." And yet, the desiring is not solely quotidian, and the poem is not satisfied to rest on the everydayness alone.

If queer theory, as it seems, is often unwilling to take up the subject of romantic love as potentially possessing a sense of meaningful futurity, queer poetry may be an apt genre to fill this lack. I cannot shake, and this is a good thing, the potentiality through intimate coupling Muñoz sees possible, one that supports his claims on queer collectivity. In "For Grace, After a Party," O'Hara

---

4 I realize these binaries are perhaps reductive, but the critical and biographical work done on both figures seems to point to these identities as rather static throughout their respective lifetimes.

is initially coy about his feelings for Hartigan: "Last night in the warm spring air while I was / blazing my tirade against someone who doesn't / interest / me, it was love for you that set me / afire, / and isn't it odd?" But the poem, harkening back to the sonnet form, contains a turning volta where the poet becomes more explicit about his strange feelings, describing Hartigan, matter-of-factly, as "someone you love." Love is not, despite the fact Hartigan and O'Hara slept with other people, sometimes the same men, an inaccurate, albeit strange with queer potentiality, adjective to describe the feelings between the two. Hartigan explains, "We fell in love... I think Frank as a homosexual was really unusual in his amount of love for a few women... that's something I've never encountered." The sentiment here, through both O'Hara's poem and Hartigan's proclamation, is breathtaking; I know many contemporary queer theorists would be all-too-quick to dismiss it, rolling their eyes and heaving a heavy sigh, but what I see, a sight the work of Muñoz has made viable, is a great potentiality for a very human, queer futurity.

Because the poem gets read again and again after O'Hara's premature death in 1966, the queer coupling of man and woman, O'Hara and Hartigan, becomes wrought and rewrought in a horizon of futurity the poem itself—where the "warm weather / is holding" and continues to hold indefinitely—can certainly imagine a historical horizon that will come to include Stonewall, the AIDS crisis, the proliferation of queer theory in the academy, and the ongoing fight for queer recognition in both the neoliberal marketplace and body politic. As we understand it through the poem, O'Hara and Hartigan's kinship is not unlike the relationship Sedgwick had with the gay poet Michael Lynch, a relationship understood through matching eyeglasses the two intimates wore and memorialized through Sedgwick's MLA address and subsequent essay "White Glasses." Therein, Sedgwick—with her breath crushing upon what could only be called romantic love—questions their identities:

> And the I who met Michael and fell in love with his white glasses? It was nobody simpler than the handsome and complicated poet and scholar I met in him; it was a queer but long-married young woman whose erotic and intellectual life were fiercely transitive, shaped by a thirst for knowledges and identifications that might cross the barriers of what seemed my identity.

We have already learned Shakespeare's sonnets are about the love one feels for inappropriate objects[5]. Though the love is quotidian, how revolutionary, how queer, indeed, it must be for O'Hara to write to Hartigan "it was love for you that set me afire." And further still, the queer marriage—because the idea of queer marriage seems much more queer here instead of the homo coupling we see all around us today—bed of Lynch and Sedgwick, which opens a space for desire on the horizon; "When I am in bed with Michael," Sedgwick claims, "our white glasses line up neatly on the night table and I always fantasy that I may walk away wearing the wrong ones."

Despite calls to assimilate, queers' love for inappropriate objects might yet be all around us today,

---

5 See Aranye Fradenburg superlative essay on the *Sonnets*, "Momma's Boys"

in these strange days of neoliberal ideology, too. Lisa Duggan warns of the ability for certain queer bodies to integrate towards straightness because "greater acceptance of the most assimilated, gender-appropriate, politically mainstream portions of the gay population has already occurred—in politics, media presentations, and the workplace—since the mid-1990s especially." Where Duggan sees a pessimism necessitated by neoliberalism, however, I am beginning to see a Day-Glo optimism of potentiality. Thus, I am curious: are the queer utopias we see in Shakespeare's *Sonnets*, arguably, and unabashedly in the dyads of both O'Hara-Hartigan and Sedgwick-Lynch, a model for the queerest relationship one can have in the twenty-first century? Robert McRuer argues that "if contemporary queer work is articulated to the idea of a collective movement or renaissance… it might be seen as disrupting or transforming the straight narrative and business as usual." Thus, is a relationship between a gay man and a beloved woman, an ally in aesthetic and cause and living, one of truly queer potential?

 The boy on whom I currently crush, a seemingly gay man with a girlfriend, claims his relationship as revolutionarily queer. For months, I have laughed or rolled my eyes at this. Now, however, I question: can I believe—both emotionally and theoretically—what he claims, having thought upon the work of O'Hara and later Sedgwick, both of whom may support his assertion? Can I believe this, despite the slippage of my own crush on him? I turn now to the poetic exercise—trained first as a poet and then as a theorist—to try and make sense of this, a triad of sonnets hearkening back to Shakespeare on the affections of O'Hara, Sedgwick, and myself. The trying will not result in any hard or fast answer, of course—queerness is always on the horizon. And yet, it is not in vain. We can at least conclude this: there is queer potential for futurity in these bodies, a queerness that must be at once capacious, while not leaving behind the very real bodies and antiheteronormativity they envisage. A queerness that is both then and now and yet to be.

Hibernation

I. Winter, 1952

Frank O'Hara walks into an office, complaining.
Save yourself, the Psychiatrist tells the Poet,
You can't do anything about your mother.
In queer time, Frank replaces her with Grace
Hartigan, firecracker formerly on the periphery
of the New York School painters O'Hara
considered his closest friends. She swiftly
becomes the subject of a short poem:
"For Grace, After a Party," where Frank tells
her, *it was love for you that set me / afire,
/ and isn't it odd? for in rooms full of / strangers
my most tender feelings / writhe and bear
the fruit of screaming.* The faggot, dear Frank,
has a crush on a woman, and isn't it odd?

II. Winter, 1986

It is fate: Eve Sedgwick meets Michael Lynch
at the 1986 MLA Convention. She crushes
hard, first on the signature thick, white glasses

upon his face, rushing to buy a matching pair,
and then quickly on the man behind the specs—
Michael, the poet succumbing to AIDS. Spring
comes. They fall in love. They lie together
and Eve, returning to Eden, the queer garden,
that which is always in the future, pontificates—
When I am in bed with Michael, our white glasses
line up neatly on the night table and I always
fantasy that I may walk away wearing the wrong
ones. Eve is married, yet denies no one, not
Adam, nor Michael, nor the woman bearing white.

III. Winter, 2013

And isn't odd? When I walk into a classroom,
I sit next to a different Michael? That he smiles
at me? That I read O'Hara & Sedgwick as I crush
into him, into this gay boy with an eight month
girlfriend? That I cannot touch him or be touched,
so I take him in the daylight to a coffeeshop?
That when I sit across from him as he reads,
I pretend to read, too, but instead read the map
that is his eyelashes and cheekbones and lips?
That I cannot tell where the map two boys
are reading will end? That when he removes
his glasses and places them next to my own
on the table between us, that I, for a moment,
dream I will walk away wearing the wrong ones?

THE WORST MOVIE NEVER MADE

WE OPEN ATOP A CLIFF looking out over a wooded valley. A crashed helicopter burns below and smoke rises up the limestone face, snaking through a dangling, white parachute. From above, a man shouts out, "Hello! Hello! Is anyone alive?" No one answers. The camera pans from his feet, his scuffed, but expensive Italian leather loafers, up his dusty, but well-tailored navy suit. On his lapel, an American flag pin is chipped, but light from the setting sun glints off its gold edges. "Dammit," he sighs, "Just dammit." We pan up to the actor's neck, his chin, his mouth, slightly agape, the bridge of his nose, his eyes, and finally, his hair, no messier than it ever is. He is atop this cliff because his helicopter has just crashed. He was the only one able to parachute out before impact. We open to our greatest nightmare: the President was on that helicopter and Keanu Reeves is now, cue title, *Commander in Chief*.

Keanu was born in Beirut, the son of, and I cannot express how much I love this, a geologist and a showgirl. Raised by his mother and four stepfathers, the young Keanu eventually landed in Toronto, where he excelled at hockey and got expelled from high school, from which he has never graduated. An injury prevented his professional hockey aspirations, so Reeves took up acting, at which he has excelled financially, with a current net worth of over $350 million. Keanu, however, is so magnificently horrible an actor that I have grown to love him and want to cast him in every equally horrible movie idea I fantasize about.

Reeves is constantly tasked with saving the world—*Matrix*, *Speed*, 2008's remake of *The Day the Earth Stood Still*, to name a few—so giving him our nuclear codes seems reasonable enough, especially as the United States mourns the sudden death of its President. Going against party leadership, Reeves will appoint a lovable Vice President whom he believes in, even though she doesn't believe in herself: *Girls* star Lena Dunham. Scenes featuring the two in the Situation Room, aboard Air Force One, at Camp David, will be so fabulously horrible—*Dude*, the President begins to plead, cutoff immediately by the Vice President, *Let me stop you right there because I have some feelings…*—you will not be able to look away.

My favorite game to play with friends is "If we were…," in which I throw out a movie, or band, or television show and we decide which of us is which of them. Buzzfeed, the "news outlet" that fancies itself a tastemaker, has made such quizzes wildly popular online, but I have been doing this since childhood, when Dora was Liesel, and I Rolf. In high school, Robby was Justin Timberlake, and I JC Chasez. Today Will is Narcissus and I am Echo, or Maia is Ann Perkins and I am Leslie Knope, or Bryan is Sam and I am Carrie, or any gaggle of gay men who happen to be sitting at a table for four are inevitably the *Golden Girls* (of whom I am always Rose). Tolkien argued, "Fantasy is escapist, and that is its glory," which is perhaps why he was such a fundamentalist Christian. Marilyn Monroe said she herself was a fantasy. In *A Midsummer Night's Dream*, Shakespeare tells us, "Lovers and madmen have such seething brains, / Such shaping fantasies." Lana Del Ray wants to know, "Are you in touch with all of your darkest fantasies?" In his *Philosophy*, Andy Warhol posits, "Everybody must have a fantasy." My fantasy is casting myself into real artifacts of popular culture, and casting superstars into artifacts of my imagination. This is in part, I suppose, my frustration with consumer capitalism that rewards such horrible actors; for every Sean Penn there is a Tom Cruise, for every Meryl Streep there is a Sandra Bullock.

Of course, the President's helicopter exploded under questionable circumstances. Keanu and Lena jointly address the nation, he swiping at his bangs, she pulling her ironic neon blazer awkwardly down over kitten-print tights; they promise to find the perpetrators behind these attacks. Back in the Oval Office, they ask the Secretary of State (Drew Barrymore) and National Security Advisor (Ashton Kutcher) who might be behind this? "Iran? North Korea? China?" Keanu wonders aloud. "Mr. President hey," Drew assures him, "that's crazy. But trust me. We will find the bad guys. Am I right?" Lena rolls her eyes, "Are you asking if you're right? You're supposed to be right. You're supposed to have a clue. You're the Secretary of State." Ashton interrupts her, "Whoa, whoa, whoa! Let's all just call down." Here I begin to wonder if this is fantasy or reality. Would I prefer a Reeves-Dunham presidency to Obama-Biden, Bush-Cheney, Clinton-Gore? The nightmare is I very well may.

Keanu and Barack may be perfect synonyms. I am no conservative, but I am beginning to rethink Republican attacks before Obama's 2008 election: that we mainly wanted him because he was a pretty face who could say things poignantly. Perhaps they were right; I can't imagine how, in a country with majority support for immigration reform, women's reproductive health, minimum wage increases, and improvements to infrastructure, that President Obama has done little beyond pass a half-ass health reform bill and drone the fuck out of civilians around the world. And yes, he speaks so eloquently. Every time I'm at the gym and see him on CNN, I fall back in love. I get that hopey-changey feeling which made me so excited back in 2008. I feel young again. In this way, Obama is not unlike Keanu Reeves. Describing Keanu in the title role of *Hamlet* (!) at the Manitoba Theatre Centre, *Sunday Times* critic Roger Lewis claims Reeves as "one of the top three Hamlets I have seen, for a simple reason: he *is* Hamlet." Following this performance, however, Keanu gives us one expensive joke: *The Matrix* trilogy. Whether 'tis nobler in the mind to suffer these men speaking so eloquently, just like Hamlet, only to let us down, just like Hamlet, or to begin looking beyond the surface when we choose our icons, political or cultural, is a question we must begin asking ourselves.

In my fantasy, Lena Dunham discovers who assassinated the President. After falling asleep in a Senate Rules Administration Subcommittee hearing—"Sorry guys, I binge watched *Murphy Brown* until four in the morning"—Dunham wanders to the basement of the Capitol building in search of coffee. Stopping to pee, she overhears a conversation. "Are you sure our tracks are covered?" asks the Secretary of Defense, Glenn Close. "Of course, darling. We are going to run this country once I kill the others," answers the Senate Majority Leader, Nicholas Cage, who we hear now making out with Close, both moaning, or cackling. We can never tell the difference with these two. "Ewwww," Lena texts to Keanu on her iPhone from inside the bathroom stall, "you are not going to believe this." In my fantasy, Keanu chases Cage to the top of the Washington Monument, where he asks, "Why did you do it?" Cage looks out the tiny window to the Potomac beyond, sighing, just before FBI Agents, played by the Jonas Brothers, handcuff him, "I guess I just wanted things to be better."

In my fantasy things are so bad they are actually better. Keanu Reeves is President, and Lena Dunham his quirky, lovable sidekick. Reality isn't as fun, though it's becoming equally bad, if not worse. Cue the closing credits: Keanu on the same cliff where we found him before, laying a white rose on the ground, a single tear rolling down his cheek as he looks to heaven, "Be all my sins remembered."

ON WALKING

> Running or walking, the way
> is the same. Be still. Be still.
> - Wendell Berry

NOT PAYING ATTENTION, I have walked into a river and a concrete stairwell and a parade of four-year-olds marching out of preschool, linked with rope as if they were a chain gang in route to Oz. Drunk, I have walked through a screened-in porch and on top of a Volkswagen Beetle and into the fountain at the Missouri State House in Jefferson City. In a home video from 1988, I am four and wearing a pull-up diaper with cherry red Justin boots. My mother holds the camera as I sashay towards her, left hand on hip, right flipping in a beauty queen wave. I sing, *These boots are made for walkin', and that's just what they'll do.*

...

I will write this from the screened-in porch of Will and Howard's home in upstate South Carolina. Will and Howard will not be here, but their three dogs will be—Hobbes, the alpha, keeping watch over his backyard kingdom from the corner; Tojo, the eldest, inside where the AC hums to life every time the sun breaks through the oak canopy; and Milton, my favorite, the basset hound named for the Renaissance poet whom Will studies, alternatively drooling asleep at my feet or trying to nudge his way onto my lap. Inside the house, Will's menagerie of fish swim circles in five tanks, much to Howard's consternation, come resignation, come now bemusement. While they are gone, I will feed the fish and walk the dogs and, if needed, mow the yard. I will cook and not go anywhere in the car Will and Howard have left behind because it is a stick shift and I do not know how to drive one. I will bike into town where there is a gym and coffeeshop. Or walk.

Will and Howard will escape these days in Alaska. Four months ago, they became foster parents to Caden, a boy from Ohio, with the intention of adopting him by the end of summer. But because all of us are haunted, Caden needed help neither Will nor Howard nor the State of South Carolina could provide. Ohio child services called Caden back and the moment that is now is a queer grief for a boy that is not dead, and yet is no longer here.

In his poem "Reaching Around For You," D.A. Powell addresses a boy in an orchard: *I do not mind you closing your own eyes, reclining. / Summoning the image of a lover put away. / Because virtue is hardly what either of us saved // from our separate, desperate beginnings.* Though I am here because I care for my friends, I am also here to grieve, it strikes me: my mother's bout with leukemia, my sister's worsening multiple sclerosis, another brother's death. Like Will and Howard to Alaska, like D.A. Powell to the orchard, I have come here to be alone in the country, to grieve and to walk.

...

In Old English, *walk* (from the Middle Dutch and Low

German *walken*) means loosely *to roll*, as in tossing water, one use, or another, kneading bread. In the "Miller's Tale," Chaucer favors the former, *him penkep verrayly þat he may se Noes flood come walkyng* (*Old Noah's flood come rolling like the sea*, line 3616). I quite like this antiquated turn, *walking like the sea*. I think of my brother, Marty, stepping out of his bass boat and onto a log which I, only six, could not see just below the surface of Table Rock Lake. Marty walking away from the boat and me thinking him some sort of prophet. Until he fell with a woosh off the end of the log. Until we both laughed our asses off.

...

A fish walks into a bar. The bartender says, *What do you want?* The fish croaks, *Water*.

...

Perhaps my origin is the story of the grief of others. I am the youngest of eight children, yes, but my siblings are all half. My sisters Diala and Starla are from our father's first marriage; Marty, Carla, Randy, Mike, and Jennifer, from our mother's. Duane, my father, spent his Air Force career married to Ginger. Because my father rose quickly through leadership training and veterinary school, he and Ginger drove beautiful cars and had a house full of Ethan Allen furniture. Because my father spent years away from home during the sixties and seventies, stationed in Vietnam and Okinawa and then Puerto Rico, Ginger cheated on him with my uncle and, as legend goes, my grandfather. Beverly, my mother, was married at seventeen to a man named Marvin. In the end, Marvin molested my oldest sister and beat my mother.

At nine, I found a police photo of her face, all dried blood and freshly blooming bruises, which she kept locked in the safe in her closet behind a pile of Dooney & Burke purses.

Though I don't know if this specific memory is real, I know it must be, because this is a scene I will see played on repeat through elementary school and junior high, when I would sit in the kitchen doing homework as my mother bore dirty dishes clean at the sink, humming Patsy Cline: *I go out walkin', after midnight, out in the moonlight, just like we used to do. I'm always walkin' after midnight, searchin' for you.*

...

In Washington, DC, I also do not have a car. This past May, it was stolen. Driven by three teenagers from Columbia Heights, our Northwest neighborhood, to Brookland, their Northeast one. Drunk, they jumped my Jeep Cherokee onto a sidewalk, hitting first a fourteen-year-old girl and then crashing into a nearby tree. The girl was walking to 7-Eleven for a slushie.

She died immediately, the police tell me at the station, where I am accidentally left in a room with her grieving mother, who invites me to the funeral we both know I will not attend. The insurance company gives me a rental car until a settlement is reached. I drive it forty miles into Maryland to collect whatever is left in the glove compartment. Mixed CDs from ex-boyfriends, a gift card to Barnes & Noble. It all seems so trivial, or distant, what I am doing, snapping pictures of the Jeep as my father has instructed, finding a spot of smeared blood on the front bumper. I do not replace the car. I deposit the insurance check and take to walking.

...

During chemo, my mother uses a wheelchair and calls to say, *This is going to kill me.* I text her statistics on walking to brighten her day: *In the United States, walking is 36 times more deadly than driving, 300 times more deadly than flying.* Similarly, my father takes to calling my mother Lieutenant Dan, after his favorite character from his favorite movie, *Forrest Gump.*

...

Every day here, I walk four miles to the gym as Howard's cherry red Mini Cooper sits idly in driveway. Quickly I begin to think of this walk as something born out of more than necessity. Though raised a Pentecostal, I am an atheist now with a recent, already passing, interest in Buddhism, less for its religiosity than its philosophical mores, which are so antithetical to my natural (impatient, controlling) tendencies. The Buddha is thought to have said, *No one saves us but ourselves. No one can and no one may. We ourselves must walk the path.* I am trying, mostly in vain, to not roll my eyes at shit this like.

    The walk begins with a steep hill that peaks and then descends from the scattering of houses that line Woodland Circle, pouring out onto Pendleton Road, which climbs west into Clemson via a slow, steady incline. Perhaps I feel accomplished taking this walk, like Thoreau in his 1862 essay "Walking," where he claims, *Every walk is a sort of crusade, preached by some Peter the Hermit in us, to go forth and reconquer this Holy Land from the hands of the Infidels.* As I walk I listen to NPR reports on the Israeli carpet-bombing of Palestine, and grow frustrated there is little I can do about this. I sweep the headphones from my ears and stuff them into my pockets.

Soon a black Mercedes stops and honks. *Want a ride into town?* the driver asks through the open sunroof, *Sorry. The window's broken.* Because he rarely had a legal drivers license and often pawned cars for drug money, my brother took to hitchhiking through the small towns dotting the Ozarks, places with names like Miller and Crane and Shell Knob. *If you ever wanna try it*, Marty told me when I was about ten, *just take stock of who's offerin' a ride.* I notice this Mercedes is missing a bumper and a rearview mirror. I notice that its tire is a spare and that its driver is black. When I say, *No thanks, I'm enjoying the walk*, I hate that he may think I don't want to take a ride from a black man in a beat-up Benz. I hate that I noticed he was black, registered this, and that the ghost of my brother, a racist amongst other things, will never stop haunting. *Whatever*, the driver shouts, pulling back onto the road.

This is not the only ride I will turn down on my walks into town, and I can only guess this is because my body is a body marked as harmless. With my beard shaved and my skinny shorts and my retro-hip backpack, not to mention my whiteness, I probably seem like a college boy trekking to campus. *Don't you have a car?* one woman asks with concern, her kids watching *Finding Nemo* on tiny televisions in the back of a mini-van.

When Leonard Woolf expressed concern to his wife regarding her long walks, Virginia replied, *To walk alone in London is the greatest rest.* I walk across a bridge over a muddy creek and think about bodies being where and doing what they are not supposed to, how this might be some essence of queerness, and how some of my favorite films are road-trip movies with women at their center: *Boys on the Side, Thelma & Louise, Little Miss Sunshine.*

For many gay men, to be gay is to be cosmopolitan and hold a disdain for nature. Which is maybe why I feel queer both in DC, where I live in a world of such gay men, and in these rolling hills, the place of my youth, the place I can't help but return to again and again, this South Carolina not so unlike my Missouri. I step into the ditch, pull down the branch of a towering shrub, and smell its fuchsia flowers until bees begin to swarm. These shrubs are everywhere here, and they lined my grandparents' homestead along the Gasconade River. I should know what they are, but I don't. Pulling my iPhone from my pocket, I snap a picture and upload it to Instagram, asking, *Can anyone identify these?* Lori, a lesbian who grew up in Mississippi, responds almost immediately, *Crepe myrtle. My southern lady flower lessons finally come in handy.*

By the time I reach the gym, I am drenched in sweat and ready for a shower. Unlike Thoreau, I'm not sure I've conquered anything beyond acquiring the colloquial genus of a pink roadside flower.

...

Popular music provides an extensive catalog of walking songs, many of which also contend with grieving. Ace of Base's 1992 "Don't Turn Around" and The Rolling Stones' 1978 "Don't Look Back." Patsy Cline's 1957 "Walking After Midnight." Aerosmith's 1975 "Walk This Way," which was never that interesting until Run-DMC covered it for their 1986 album *Raising Hell*. The Four Seasons' 1963 "Walk Like a Man." Johnny Cash's 1956 "Walk The Line." Marc Cohn's 1991 "Walking in Memphis," which Cher covered (horribly) in 1995. Yet, there is one tune in the American songbook that captures this country's walking spirit, its desire for hope in the face of loss, better than any other.

Ironically, it is Scottish twins Charlie and Craig Reid's hit "I'm Gonna Be (500 Miles)." Though released in the United Kingdom in August of 1988, the song did not see an American release until the summer of '93, when it appeared in *Benny & Joon*. Among cinephiles, the film is remembered for little more than making The Pretenders' song a runaway hit, now as ubiquitous to American karaoke bars as Budweiser and drunken fraternity boys ready to be the men who walk 1,000 miles just to fall down at your door.

...

After Patsy Cline died in a plane crash ninety miles outside Nashville on March 5, 1963, her grief-stricken friend June Carter was unable to attend the funeral.

The two women loved each other so deeply the love became perhaps like the complicated relationship one might have with a sibling. Both wrote of this tumultuous love, and various other sources, from Johnny Cash to Loretta Lynn, have corroborated the sentiment. The year before the plane crash, Carter told Cline she was toeing a dangerous line, taking up with married men in the small world of country music. Cline called Carter a hypocrite, asking, "What exactly do you think it is you're doing with Johnny?" I do not bring this up to hypothesize why Carter didn't attend Cline's funeral. From all the reading I've done, it seems they had reconciled and slipped into old ways by that point. But I do bring it up to say: sometimes those closest to us are capable of cutting deep with complicated motive, simultaneously pure and dark, loving and loathing. While their friends attended the funeral, June tasked herself with taking care of Patsy's young children.

This, I can certainly understand—a desire to *do* in the time of grief.

In the years before Marty committed suicide, he kept a room at our house, where he'd stay as he tried to kick the methadone habit born out of his methamphetamine dealing habit. In the months before he died, Marty seemed on the mend. He was laughing again, a boisterous laugh I also have, and working construction with our brother Randy and my father Duane. The last time I saw Marty we fought. I called him *white trash*; he called me *faggot*. A week later, Marty was dead, and we would learn just how adept he'd become at hiding his slip back into the hell of hard drugs. I refused to go to my brother's funeral. In the weeks that followed, my mother in bed, my father absent in memory, I took to walking to the grocery store, asking for cardboard boxes, packing Marty's things (clothes, splattered with the paint of a carpenter, and albums, mostly AC/DC), and stacking these boxes in a corner of our tool shed.

...

Will and Howard's home is nothing astonishing, a split level ranch on a forest road outside of Pendleton, South Carolina, about four miles from Clemson University, where Will teaches Renaissance literature and Howard has a law practice. The house itself: four bedrooms, two bathrooms, and a basement rec room, where a 125-gallon fish tank anchors one wall. While Howard and Will are in Alaska, I feed these fish daily and think how this might be one manifestation of love.

I love the screened-in porch on the back of their home. And this is strange, because it, too, is nothing astonishing: a set of comfortable rattan patio furniture that always makes me think of the living room from *Golden Girls* and a four-and-a-half foot statue of a rooster made from salvaged metal signs. The plume of its tail is a Coca-Cola sign, and though the piece is perhaps kitschy, I love it. The days I am spending alone here, two of the three dogs—Hobbes, the alpha of the group, and Milton, the basset who rarely leaves my side—hold court on the porch, where I sit reading and writing, sometimes napping, sometimes listening to old recordings of Johnny Cash and June Carter, research for another writing project. Beyond the porch's screens, the yard is parched this year, which embarrasses Will; normally, he takes great pride in having nice grass and landscaped flowers in this climate which rejects non-native forest growth. In the past months, however, as spring became summer, Will spent his days and nights with Caden, the son so non-native to any environment his pruning required constant diligence. A border of pin oaks line the yard, punctuated by a single, tall, scrubby pine. I've always been drawn to this anomalous tree and when packing to come see Will and Howard, I hum "Wagon Wheel" by Old Crow Medicine Show, *Headed down south to the land of the pines, thumbin' my way outta North Caroline.*

Why do I love their porch so? It is like my childhood home, a brown ranch on Slim Wilson Boulevard in Nixa, Missouri, where a sun porch faced a line of pin oaks punctuated by a single willow. Topographically, upstate South Carolina is not unlike the Missouri Ozarks, lands of unmanageable soils. But for all the reasons Will and Howard's porch may reminisce of my parents', it is also very different. The similar comfort is one of familiarity; the difference being that here, I feel the comfort of the absence of my family. And yet this explanation seems ultimately failed, along the lines of student essays—*this text is both the same and different as*—Will and I have come to mock.

Today I have been reading Sheryl St. Germain's newest book, *Navigating Disaster: Sixteen Essays of Love and a Poem of Despair*. Sheryl writes often of New Orleans, her homeland, but "this collection of essays," she explains, "begins in a place, like New Orleans, of extremity and strong personality: southeast Alaska, where I traveled alone a few years ago… because it seemed in some ways as far away as I could get from Louisiana, and at a time I needed to put distance between myself and my family." Will and Howard have traveled to Alaska, I suspect, for many of the same reasons: to be together in a place that is not this home of a fractured family. I have traveled to Will and Howard's home to care for the dogs and fish of my friends, certainly, but also to mourn a complicated year for my own blood family.

Tonight, reading in the yellowing light of early evening, I hear a bird cooing from the pine tree, a bird whose call I recognize from the few hunting trips I took with my brothers. It is the mourning dove—I open my laptop and confirm this on YouTube—abundant in both the Carolinas and the Ozarks. It is the bird my brothers hunted, but I refused to shoot as a child. My brothers took to calling me Warden, after the song "Folsom Prison Blues," where Johnny Cash sings, *When I was just a baby, my mama told me son, always be a good boy, don't ever play with guns.* When Marty chose to kill himself, he did it with a .22 gauge shotgun propped on one foot so the other foot could toe the trigger, the barrels resting in his open mouth not unlike the kiss of a beloved.

...

Descartes walks into a bar. The bartender asks, *Can I get you a drink?* Descartes replies, *I think not*, and disappears.

...

In Middle English, *walk* shifts to its present use, *to move about, to journey*. In his series of sonnets, "The Visions of Petrarch," (1529) Edmund Spenser tells of his muse: *On hearbs and floures she walked pensiuely.* In her 1788 novel *Emmeline,* Charlotte Turner Smith muses on her heroine: *Miss Mowbray was walked out, as was her custom, very early, no one knew whither.* In 1974, Adrienne Rich amuses a lover: *Walking the City of Love, so cold we warmed our nerves with wine at every all-night café.* I used to beg, *Dad, can we take a walk?* I never knew why he answered, *Walking is for girls.* My father and I? We hiked mountains, we paddled rivers, we ran bases. At night, we might *exercise* the dogs. The Four Seasons were wrong, my father might say, one cannot walk like a man.

...

Leaving the Pendleton town square, I walk back west toward Will and Howard's. Google Maps leads me to a winding road that cuts through a couple of gullies before ending at the turn north onto Woodland Circle. This road is mostly unpopulated, its ditches overgrown with kudzu, that invasive species that creeps along many roads in upstate South Carolina, but now, too, my native Ozarks. It chokes out all other life: wildflowers and grasses first, then bushes, and eventually trees as mighty as sentinel oak or maple. I happen upon a bend in the road, where a group of white men sit on lawn chairs smoking cigarettes and drinking Miller Lite. From the other direction, a motorcycle in need of a new muffler approaches and one of the men stumbles up to greet it at the end of a gravel driveway. He waves at me, *Howdy*, and pulls a small baggie from his pocket, which the woman on the back of the motorcycle takes, handing him a wad of crumpled bills, before riding off past me.

No, I am not scared on most city streets, but at three in the afternoon my heart rate quickens and I begin to sweat on this back road of upstate South Carolina. I am suddenly aware of how stupid I am, in my very gay cutoff shorts and hip vintage t-shirt, iPhone and Jack Spade wallet dangling from pockets, backpack holding a MacBook. There is a variety of hydrangea I've never seen growing beside the trailer. I open my mouth to ask the man about them. But I stop myself, thinking better of being the gay boy asking about flora and fauna. I have seen my brother, a meth dealer and user himself, pummel his wife Gracia in the face, knocking her to the ground where he kicked her again and again—*You dirty whore 'spic!*—until someone could pull them apart, all because she asked a question and he was rolling. No, I am not scared on most city streets, but I am scared of my own brother, of his ghost I see in every man sitting outside that trailer, their baggies of meth, their days passing the same as yesterday and tomorrow.

...

Shakespeare walks into a bar and asks the barman for a beer. *I can't serve you,* says the barman, *You're bard!*

...

Like its songbook, our culture also contains many walking films. Like walking songs, many of these films revel in grief, often masked in the form of a quest (what is grief, if not part of a quest). Released in Technicolor on the first day of 1939, the most famous walking movie must be *The Wizard of Oz*, where four unlikely friends seek out the thing they have lost (Scarecrow, a brain; Tin Man, a heart; Cowardly Lion, courage; and Dorothy, queer icon that she is, longing for home). Because their budget precluded horses, 1975's *Monty Python and the Holy Grail* brings us a group of knights trotting along English roads as if on horseback, followed by a man banging together coconut shells. This century brings us *The Lord of the Rings* trilogy, which feels, in my humble opinion, like a 47-hour walk through some boring woods that are supposed to seem harrowing.

The most atrocious walking movie, however, has to be

2002's *A Walk to Remember*, though perhaps it captures the walking-grieving compendium best. On the film's IMBD website, Scott of Milwaukee gives this synopsis of the film—

> In a coastal North Carolinian small town in the mid 1990's, a boy [Landon] from the popular but troubled undirected group of students gets busted, and for punishment, you guessed it, has to do community service activities which include the high school's spring play. This throws him in with the minister's daughter [Jamie], you guessed it, the mousy seemingly awkward yet beautiful girl with an angelic heart, and she sings too. They grow hesitantly closer than their previous adversarial relationship as old bonds are tested and new awarenesses are inspired. A couple twists occur as the story concludes.

I hate to ruin it, but the twists center around two revelations. First, Jamie (played by none other than pop star Mandy Moore) brings Landon (an admittedly handsome, if not tiresome, Shane West) back to the most banal, secularized form of Jesus loving (under a soundtrack chock-full of Christian rock bands like Jars of Clay and Switchfoot). Second, we come to find out Jamie, whose darkening eye shadow denotes her growing frailty throughout the film, is dying of leukemia. By the time this is revealed, however, Landon is in love with Jamie, and she him, so they decide (as any sensible high school senior would do), to get married. A phantasmagorical ceremony follows, performed by Jamie's minister-father during which Jamie wears her dead mother's wedding dress.

Jamie's walk down the aisle becomes one of the many walks prominent in the movie, all of which, we are lead to believe, are ones to remember. In the most memorable, the film's penultimate scene, we find Landon, four years older and now on his way to medical school, walking through a beachside nature preserve where he and Jamie went on their first date. Landon walks then to Jamie's father's door, whining that Jamie didn't get to finish her bucket list, topped by the dream, *witness a miracle*. "I'm sorry she never got her miracle," Landon says, prompting the father to conclude, "She did. It was you." At this point I fully expected Jamie to leap out of the closet à la Christ's resurrection. But no, Landon just walks away.

...

Unlike *walk*, the Middle English verb *grieve* is simply from the French *grever*, *to put a strain upon*, which is itself simply a derivative of the Latin *gravāre*, meaning *heavy*. In Wycliffite's *Bible* (1382), Jesus comes upon his disciples asleep in the garden (Matthew 26:43) with heavy, grieved, eyes: *And eftsone he came, and foonde hem slepynge; forsothe her eȝen weren greued*. Three centuries later, a common usage was *grieve* as in assault. In his 1651 *Leviathan*, Thomas Hobbes contends, *Nature hath armed living creatures, some with teeth, some with horns, and some with hands, to grieve an enemy*. Likewise, the English poet William Cowper queerly predicts Sarah Palin's sense of humor in 1782: *A Christian's wit is inoffensive light, A beam that aids but never grieves the sight*. But this use of grieve is outward, not the use most common today. *Grieue not the holy Spirit of God*, beseeches King James' 1611 translation of Ephesians. In 1667, Milton tells how

God *Griev'd at his heart, when looking down he saw / The whole Earth fill'd with violence.* In his 1860 commentary *The Minor Prophets*, Oxford's Dr. Edward Bouverie Pusey claims, *The Holy Spirit they have grieved away.*

Somewhere, we stopped grieving God. In his 1951 villanelle, Dylan Thomas posits, *Wild men who caught and sang the sun in flight, / And learn, too late, they grieved it on its way, / Do not go gentle into that good night.* Matthew Dickman's 2008 poem "Slow Dance" replies, *There is no one to save us / because there is no need to be saved.* I am not sure if this is comfort, but I know Hobbes needs a long walk tonight after two days of rain. That I need the unresolve of a poem. Of walking, of grieving. Of this dog pawing my leg, warning he will piss all over the linoleum again if we do not get moving.

RIDING IN CARS WITH BROTHERS

> If you would win the hard identity
> Of brothers—a long race for men to run
> - Allen Tate

ON OCTOBER 3, 2004, the EA Sports 500 took place at the Talladega Superspeedway. That humid Sunday, 172,138 ticketed attendees filled the stands of the largest track used by the National Association for Stock Car Auto Racing, NASCAR, though the number is conservative given the tens of thousands who pack the miles of abandoned farmland that surround the track, tailgating and camping and raising cane. It is not unlike a Dixie Woodstock, and the lore goes that on race day, Talladega becomes the most populated city in Alabama. On October 3, 2004, I was a college freshman—young and awkward and uncomfortably queer—sitting on the searing metal of stadium seating as stock car drivers looped 188 laps around the 2.66 mile track, often in excess of 200 miles per hour. Such speed is a dizziness that blurs, or perhaps revises, memory.

I had traveled from Missouri to Alabama as a concession. My mother guilted my father and brother, Randy, into taking me for my birthday. I did not want to go, really, and they probably would have preferred going without me. But these men asked so earnestly. Nineteen and weird and on the verge—like every nineteen year old, it seems—of some great self-revelation, I wasn't in the position to turn down the attention. Our trip itself? Unmemorable but for flashes. Ten hours in Randy's Chevy Lumina listening to an endless loop of Johnny Cash, Elvis Presley, and Alabama. *Song, song of the South. Sweet potato pie and I shut my mouth. Gone, gone with the wind. There ain't nobody looking back again.* During the race itself, reading *Catcher in the Rye* and Dad spilling beer onto the paperback. Drinking my first beer with Dad and Randy, neither of whom drink in front of Mom. Going to a local mall for dinner at Applebee's. Finding a cruisy bathroom at the mall. Finding a boy at one of the urinals. Finding his cock as he finds mine and we masturbate into the pool of piss and pink disinfectant disc. My brother finding me in the bathroom just as the boy and I are cumming, and never speaking of this. Later, after many more beers at the house we had rented for the weekend, skinny dipping in the cedar-lined hot tub with my brother and feeling his hand brush my knee. Then again. His eyes closed because he is married and straight and also my brother and we are drunk.

In his Gospel, St. John claims, "my Father's house has many rooms." In the Gospel no one has written of my family—*my Father's house has many rooms. Rooms in which camps segregate.* A house divided against itself can, it turns out, stand, however shakily. In my Father's house there are many rooms, and I am usually in the sewing room with Mom and my sister, Jennifer, drinking Diet Coke, watching HGTV, and *Carrying on like we ain't got a care in the world*, Mom says. The river of a family's genetics rarely flows evenly. It eddies and meanders, dams and trickles. Jennifer and I, for instance, are both extroverts like our mother. Our big, strange laughs, guffaws, sound like birds in pain. We are both teachers, both hold graduate degrees, and are both vegetarians. Physically, however, I look most like Randy. We are both slim, but not waifs, with the pale skin of our Welsh blood mixed with darker Hopi Indian. Our facial hair borders on red and our smiles are crooked, turning higher on the left side of our faces than the right. And because we were drunk in a hot tub and we are brothers and he is Randy and our memory revises, the last thing I remember of that night is accidentally tickling his thigh, leaning in to kiss my brother and his smile, like my own, making the kiss lopsidedly sweet and strange and familiar.

No man in my family should drink. We are, in this way, very Southern indeed: taken by muggy nights to points of excess. My father, now sober, is an alcoholic and my mother will not stand for this in her house. My other brothers— Marty and Mike, both dead—have spent so much time in and out of emergency rooms, rehab, and prison, it seems a moot point to drone on about them. Randy and I know our limits and rarely pass them. But on a night in a hot tub after your brother has watched you cum in a public bathroom with another boy beside you, you will both want to drink. And when you kiss you will want to both remember that the world was one of possibility then, but not want to remember the particulars. You will both be thankful for the line of demarcation a blackout provides. A before and after, a known and unknown.

Why did I desire—*and sometimes desire still?*—my own brother, the one I most closely resemble, though we are so vastly different. He, a father, a builder of palatial, custom homes for the wealthy. Me, a writer, an almost doctor of American literature. Is this an exercise in queer narcissism? When I visit home during Christmas my first year of graduate school, Randy asks—a question he has never asked before or since—"What have you been reading?" I'd been reading Freud, who has much to say on the subject of desire and the ego, of course. Is ours, this relationship between Randy and I, silently volatile, an example of, as Freud describes, "very intense feelings of rivalry giving rise to aggressive desires, which, after they have been surmounted, are succeeded by love for the object that was formerly hated or by an identification with it?"

I know we sat alone and sweating in a hot tub in the middle of Alabama, where we were, briefly, just brothers at a NASCAR race. But I don't remember, or cannot remember, what happens until the next day. When, hungover but drinking again under the hot Sunday sun, we watched Jeff Gordon wreck somewhere around the 150th lap, a wreck that would ultimately cost him the race. I remember later trying to make this a metaphor for what had happened and not happened the night before as we drove home through the lowlands of western Tennessee. I remember how strange it was that Cole Porter was on the radio. How he sang, "Read and let read, write and let write. Love and let love, bite and let bite." How strange it is now that I think of Talladega, and Randy, and my sudden, quick waning love for NASCAR. My queer love for NASCAR, much like my love for the South it represents, and my brother…how I think about all this at a hip coffeeshop in Washington, DC—a city that, like myself, has a complicated relationship with its Southern roots. This shop serves coffee in excess of $5 a cup alongside vegan pie. Today, I order the sweet potato, and wistfully, shut my mouth.

COLBY KELLER FOR PRESIDENT

WE ARE LEAVING THE CITY behind in the dream. We are leaving the city behind and lying upon the edge of a pool on a cliff overlooking the ocean. In Mexico, the city is behind us and Colby is reading poetry as I float on a raft: *We two boys together clinging, / One the other never leaving*. On the screen, the scene is fleeting, offering a CockyBoys™ seven-day trial membership for $14.95.

...

I am waiting at Dooby's, a hip Baltimore café, for my friend Colby, whom I know quite well digitally, but have yet to meet in real life. Such is contemporary humanity. Colby Keller is undoubtedly one of the world's biggest gay porn stars, his digital footprint like his bodily footprint, huge, distinct, and to many, instantly recognizable. Colby is also one of the smartest—not to mention kindest—men I know; he holds an MFA in sculpture from the Maryland Institute College of Art (MICA), one of the nation's top art schools, and he reads Marxist theory and contemporary poetry voraciously. Here I lay bare a bias: it was initially difficult to reconcile the Colby I knew from his porn, those images of a chiseled Adonis sweating onto the back of a hipster as they fuck, with the Colby that sat across from me, talking of Whitman and what his poetic might mean in the age of neoliberalism. I have begun to write this essay many times, but my friend Will, upon examining these attempts, tells me I'm basically saying, *Look! The porn star can read!*

That is not my intention.

I met Colby in real life at a time, the second decade of the twenty-first century, both interesting to be a gay man and for me to be a gay man entering the discipline of queer theory. Regarding the former, homosexual lobbyists had "fought" for and were earning a number of "rights," most visibly the ability for homos to serve openly in the military and to marry in a growing number of states and in the city I now call home, Washington, DC. Regarding the latter, the twenty-first century has birthed an often-visceral divide between the academic discipline of queer theory and the mainstream homosexual lobby, represented most prominently by the behemoth Human Rights Campaign. The mainstream homosexual lobby paints academics who criticize them as elitist and out of touch; queer-minded academics paint the homosexual lobby as shortsighted and concerned only in furthering capitalism and its most protected class, white men. To me, Colby Keller has come to be an image, a metaphor, for how these two groups might bridge their aspirations: Colby is a man, after all, visually concerned for his own sexual desires, but also connected to a larger queer politic that recognizes the social needs of others.

...

If a thesis here is necessary: queerness is not threatened most by heteronormativity, but by homonormativity, not by people outside of the LGBT community, but by the most powerful class, white gay men, therein. If a theorem here might be helpful to understand the implication of this: queer ≠ gay.

...

Like a dog in heat, the first question begs: if queerness is not *only* a synonym for homosexuality—reclaimed, like *bitch*, from a violent slur to a glittery badge of honor—then what is it? The short answer: few agree. Divides in defining *queer* begin with an understanding of sexuality as either essential or socially constructed; on one hand, we have Lady Gaga espousing essentialism, *Baby you were born this way*, and on the other, we have Michel Foucault yelling, *Fuck essentialism! We, neither nature nor birth, determine our own sexualities*. The contemporary homosexual lobby—what Lisa Duggan calls Gay, Inc.—builds its case on essentialism: if we are born this way, then the state cannot discriminate against us. Within state-sanctioned institutions (marriage, the military, taxes), Gay, Inc. finds freedom.

Along with a majority of scholars, I find this shortsighted; we argue that if sexuality is a construct, rather than a given, we can determine our own lives and freedoms outside the purview of the state. Kevin Floyd argues, "*Queer* is not merely a terminological abstraction; it also refers to a form of social abstraction." As such, we find queerness not limited to our individual sexual identities, but malleable to describing our politics and ways of thinking about and improving the world. White gay men, who like white men generally tend to think they deserve everything, find this frustrating because here queerness might not place their desires first. To many scholars, a gay man could be homosexual without being queer. Believe me, this is not popular to say to drunk dudes grabbing your ass at Pride or to self-righteous men on Facebook.

...

Then again, here I, too, am being self-righteous. Imagine the expert in the law of Luke 10 presently as a young queer theorist. Imagine me asking Jesus, "And who is queer?" Imagine Jesus slapping me across the face, "Bitch, please."

...

"Fuck you and fuck your PhD you elitist douchebag," a man messaged me the week before Christmas, 2014. That fall had been dominated by the murder of two Black men by white police officers without cause. Eighteen-year-old Michael Brown had been gunned down by Darren Wilson in suburban St. Louis on August 9; a grand jury failed to take Wilson to trial. On December 3, a grand jury also failed to indict New York City police officers for strangling Eric Garner; this failure, despite video footage of Garner telling police officers "I can't breathe" eleven times before he lost consciousness, at which point the officers failed to perform CPR. As a nation, we were failing. We had been failing Black citizens without reprieve for over 300 years. Following these deaths, protests broke out across the country, some of the most visible of which took place in Washington, DC.

Protesters had taken to blocking major thoroughfares in our nation's capital, most prominently a section of the I-395 Beltway, one of the busiest sections of highway in the United States. An acquaintance posted about this on Facebook, remarking, "This is wrong! Why are they disrupting LIFE?" I was surprised. This man is gay; he holds a masters degree in the humanities; he is an ASL interpreter and works in deaf advocacy. How could he be so critical of protests to injustice? I commented on his post: "Do you think the disruption to Washingtonians' lives might pale in comparison to the violence Black Americans face at the hands of police every day?" He responded, "That doesn't give them the right to block traffic unlawfully. They should lobby like we did to get marriage equality." Others chimed in. Called me an elitist. Called him a racist. A digital riot ensued. But, a brief pause, because

...

Queer theory as queer politic offers to coalesce us into a public, intelligent working group of reformers for issues of race alongside sex and gender! Richard Thompson Ford explains his excitement to this end: "Queer theory offered a way to take race politics back from the professionals. It had—at least it seemed to me—a closer and fresher connection with the everyday life of a counterculture, with its contradictions, its sweaty struggles, its passions, its screwups, its street styles and fashion faux pas. Queer theory, with its open-handed conflicts and negotiations between gay men, lesbians, trannies, butch and lipstick lesbians, tops, bottoms, clean-shaven Chelsea boys and bearded burly *bears*." This praxis has both political and personal implications, because one of the greatest facets of queer life outside of homonormative gayness is also our ability to define our own relationships.

...

It is true that sometimes all queer bonding asks for is a recognition, like that between Colby and me, or that between Frank O'Hara and his intimate, the painter Grace Hartigan. In a poem to Hartigan, O'Hara surmises this queer recognition: "And someone you love enters the room / and says wouldn't / you like the eggs a little // different today? / And when they arrive they are / just plain scrambled eggs."

...

This desire for plain scrambled eggs is not my way of robbing queerness of sex. I love sex. I have had sex with some of my closest friends, or been intimate in a way that renders others under an assumption we are fucking. Michel Foucault explains,

> A way of life can be shared among individuals of different ages, status, and social activity. It can yield intense relations not resembling those that are institutionalized. It seems to me that a way of life can yield a culture and an ethics. To be "gay," I think, is not to identify with the psychological traits and the visible masks of the homosexual but to try and define and develop a way of life.

In a poem, Will, my dearest queer brother, once described how we could "make love without having sex," and try as I might, this is the closest descriptor of our friendship, one that has and continues to confound the gay men around us, to whom I want to often say, *Fuck off.*

...

Which is to say, I think all gay men, myself included, battle constantly to remain open to new ways of being instead of embracing conservative, homonormative values. Eve Sedgwick contends "that 'queer' can refer to: the open mesh of possibilities, gaps, overlaps, dissonances and resonances, lapses and excesses of meaning when the constituent elements of anyone's gender, of anyone's sexuality aren't made (or can't be made) to signify monolithically." The mainstream gay lobby, representing the most privileged class of queer society, would like us to think of our lives—both our sexual and interpersonal—monolithically; they would like us to act as upstanding straights do in order to gain the rights that in no way should be tied to one's ability to couple or to be *normal*.

And surely part of living queerly is the giving over of oneself to Otherness, because as Judith Butler famously opines,

...

"Let's face it. We are undone by each other." Butler links desire and grieving, implying that if we can be undone by each other, we can also be radically redone, which is how I've begun to think of my queer friendships, such as my relationships with Will or with Colby, who in the spring of 2014, undertook a project titled "Everything But Lenin."

Evicted from his Baltimore studio, Colby decided to leave Charm City, where he had lived for the last decade through graduate school and his rise to porn superstardom, to travel the United States. "Everything But Lenin" was his attempt to remove the accumulated possessions from his life, in which he gave away everything but a metal plaque of the Communist icon to create, by both the giving and the object's new "life," literally thousands of art installations. Colby understood, as I think many of us suspect, that things have the ability to possess us just as much, perhaps more, than we have the ability to possess them. Again Butler speaks of our gender and sexuality as things, positing that "neither of these is precisely a possession, but both are to be understood as modes of being dispossessed, ways of being for another, or indeed, by virtue of another." If gayness is a thing we can both know and possess, through the law and the accumulation of shiny, glittery things vis-a-vis the capitalism that law seeks, above all else, to protect and serve, then perhaps queerness is that which we can never know, the thing that, every day, can dispossess us from ourselves. Like this we are undone and redone ad infinitum.

...

In the beginning was the Word, and the Word was with us, and the Word was *queer*. So to quote Fräulein Maria, "Let's start at the very beginning, a very good place to start." Queer poses, and has long posed, a linguistic conundrum; the term can be used as not only noun, but also adjective, verb, and adverb. The earliest (easily) recognizable use of queer comes from the Anglo-Norman and Middle French verb, meaning *to ask, to inquire, to question*, from which we yield the modern *query*. In the early sixteenth century, the verb *to question* reached an answer, it seems: *strange, odd, peculiar, eccentric. Also: of questionable character; suspicious, dubious.* This is the root of the connection between *queer* and *homosexual*, though the written usage as such does not enter the lexicon until much later, in an 11 November 1914 article of the *Los Angeles Times*: "He said that the Ninety-six Club was the best; that it was composed of the 'queer' people... He said that the members sometimes spent hundreds of dollars on silk gowns, hosiery, etc.... At these 'drags' the 'queer' people have a good time."

This use of queer as *peculiar* leads to its use as *bad; contemptible, worthless; untrustworthy; disreputable* and *to make a fool of, ridicule; to swindle, cheat; to get the better of. Later also: to puzzle, flummox, confound, baffle.* The final entry given by the *Oxford English Dictionary* predicts the more recent conundrum both homosexuals and theorists have with *queer*, simply self-defining: *that which is queer (in various senses)*. In short: queer is queer.

...

Outside of academia and far-left activism, *queer* has become generally synonymous with *gay*. Linguistically, this may be dangerous because the contemporary gay lobby puts forward a very narrow definition of what is acceptable gayness, which they call queerness, but is anything but. Which is to say, to be gay in the twenty-first century is to be a white, wealthy, urban, cisgendered man. By this reasoning, the gay man of today is often not unlike the conservative man: concerned first for his own needs and second for the protection of a *normal* society.

...

To live in Washington is to learn the technique of avoidance. My office sits at the corner of 22nd and I Streets Northwest, an intersection at the heart of George Washington University frequented by nonprofit canvassers. Colleagues and I avoid walking by these people if possible, which it rarely is, or at least avoid any engagement with them beyond, *I'm sorry*, as we rush by not listening to whatever cause they are selling. The Human Rights Campaign (HRC) keeps a steady stream of "fundraising associates" at this intersection, mostly young gay men, who think working for the HRC buys some credibility, and young women, who look like their young gay colleagues dressed them.

 Recently, a cute guy asked if I wanted to become an HRC member as I walked to the Metro. "No, sorry," I said, but he jogged to catch up: "Do you not care about gay rights?" I stopped and in no uncertain terms, barked a treatise on why the HRC does not represent my political interests nor those of a queer politic writ-large. Their contemporary politicking has centered primarily around three issues: 1) the overturning of "Don't Ask, Don't Tell," thus allowing gays to serve openly in the United States military; this, a short-sighted politic indeed, as it asks for gays to serve in an innately homophobic, war-mongering machine instead of questioning the very existence, or size, of that machine. 2) the expansion of state-sanctioned marriage to gay and lesbian couples on both the state and national level; this, a short-sighted politic indeed, as it asks for gays and lesbians to allow the government entrance into their relationships in order to receive certain rights or benefits, such as health care and tax breaks, which should be allowed to everyone. 3) the ranking of companies as "gay friendly" on an annual

Corporate Equality Index.

This last point drives me especially bat-shit crazy, as it labels otherwise-horrible multi-national corporations as stellar places for gays to work. The HRC's 2015 list includes oil companies reaping havoc on the environment (Chevron, Exxon-Mobil); pharmaceutical companies more concerned with inflated profits than providing essential medicines to the sick domestically and abroad (GlaxoSmithKline, Pfizer); defense companies developing weapons allowing the United States and its allies to takeover countries and their resources (Lockheed Martin, Northrop Grumman); financial conglomerates which caused the 2008 global economic crisis and used subsequent public bailouts to pay bonuses to already-top wealth holders (Goldman Sachs, JPMorgan Chase); and, because of its political maneuvering and take-over of both the world's farming and food, what many have referred to as the most evil corporation on the face of the earth: Monsanto. And yet, because these places train employees in diversity, or give partner benefits, or most likely, financially support the gay rights lobby, they are deemed the best places for us to work. Sara Ahmed argues, "A queer phenomenology would involve an orientation toward queer, a way to inhabit the world that gives support to those whose lives and loves make them appear oblique, strange, and out of place." The HRC's support of these companies seems not only short-sighted, but also dangerous in making impossible what Ahmed rightfully argues a queer politic should encompass; here we find American gays happy to work at a place making weapons to kill gays in Palestine, Afghanistan, Iraq, etc., etc.

...

Although sometimes queerness revels in death and mourning and the past, without, and this is key, calling for death in the present. Lee Edelman names this the "death drive," explaining "the queer, in the order of the social, is called forth to figure: the negativity opposed to every form of social viability." If mainstream homonormativity focuses on our bright shiny futures, which I am not claiming is in and of itself bad, then queerness may, in turn, mourn the unnameable. My participation in Colby's "Everything But Lenin" included my taking of a plain, black box. Inside, a plastic bag contained remnant ashes of his father, for whom Colby is named, who had died the year before. Here queerness both mourned our past, the death of Colby's literal father, and recognized a queer future through Colby and I embracing one another and the hardships which we have endured, are enduring, and will endure. Ours is a death drive that does not deny the past but recognizes that, as José Muñoz preaches, "The future is queerness' domain."

...

And though the future is queerness' domain, we have to live in the present, to contend with queerness—both a linguistic and a political and a bodily problem—in the present. David Halperin contends that, "Queer is by definition whatever is at odds with the normal, the legitimate, the dominant. There is nothing in particular to which it necessarily refers. It is an identity without an essence." So if a queer politic refers to capacious care for *all* those at odds with the normal, the legitimate, and the dominant, a queer friendship may be finding that common bond of illegitimacy within the Other. In Colby, for instance, I see a reflection of my anger at mainstream gay politics and further, the type of ennui I feel at my own comrades' refusal to question such institutions, or to bitch, or to become the bitch of a dominant politic in order to undue it. As the poet Jericho Brown commands, "Speak to me in a lover's tongue—/ Call me your bitch, and I'll sing the whole night long." Perhaps queerness is exactly this: Longing for the lover's sweet-speaking tongue to call you, *Bitch*.

...

To willingly be called *Bitch* is to relegate oneself to the beta position. Queer theory recognizes there is not only sexual, but also social power in this. The mainstream gay lobby, the rank and file of the Human Rights Campaign and its numerous subsidiaries and followers permeated with a "me, me, ME" mentality, fighting first and foremost for their own rights and desires, may well learn from this willing relegation. Which is why,

...

I dream of Colby reading Whitman, twisting beard between forefinger and thumb: "I will plant companionship thick as trees along all the rivers of America, and along the shores of the great lakes, and all over the prairies, / I will make inseparable cities with their arms about each other's necks, / By the love of comrades, / By the manly love of comrades."

I dream of a Queer America, which is why I want

Colby Keller to run for president. My friend embodies queerness; he does not rob it of sex, as the conservative right would do; nor does he rob it of a capaciously queer, revolutionary politic, as the mainstream gay lobby would do, asking us not to question capitalism, or consumerism, or militarism, but instead to accept these on our path to homonormativity. I can imagine Colby, perhaps replete in cowboy hat and chaps, reading from *The Queer Nation Manifesto* at a campaign rally —

> Being queer means leading a different sort of life. It's not about the mainstream, profit-margins, patriotism, patriarchy or being assimilated. It's not about executive directors, privilege and elitism. It's about being on the margins, defining ourselves; it's about gender-fuck and secrets, what's beneath the belt and deep inside the heart; it's about the night. Being queer is "grass roots" because we know that everyone of us, every body, every cunt, every heart and ass and dick is a world of pleasure waiting to be explored. Everyone of us is a world of infinite possibility.

We live in a time when queerness is not threatened most by heteronormativity, but by homonormativity, not by people outside of the LGBT community, but by the most powerful class, white gay men, therein. But every one of us is a world of infinite possibility. Colby Keller for President: Queerness for All.

BRITNEY, OUR LADY OF PERPETUITY

> toward dinnertime, you do what you came to do:
>   *Ziggy Stardust* and *American Graffiti*.
> Funny the things that save our lives.
> - Heather McNaugher

"**BULLSHIT**," Paul says, twisting his red beard between his thumb and forefinger, "Andy would be obsessed with Beyoncé. Britney is too much of a mess."

"But that's the point!" I exclaim, "Andy loved tragic women. Jackie, Liz, Edie. Britney would be his Factory girl, don't you think?" Paul shakes his head, laughs in a breathy way out of a corner of his mouth, a gesture that makes me smile, too. We're on the happy side of drunk, talking about Andy Warhol and who would be his muse if the painter were alive today. It's summer in Pittsburgh, the City of Bridges—well over four hundred of them; the City of Champions; The Steel City; the city where I've come to graduate school, to learn to poem.

I hate sestinas. I hate writing in any type of poetic form that requires such repetition; a sestina is 39 lines long, six stanzas of six lines that use the same end words over and over. It's an obsessive form, yes, not unlike the paintings of Andy Warhol, the Campbell's tomato soup cans, for instance, or his portraits of Marilyn Monroe, so many paintings all based on a single publicity photo. When I came to graduate school, my first poetry workshop was led by Peter, a kind man who loves Pittsburgh, Andy

Warhol, and sestinas. When he assigned us to write a sestina, I wrote "Britney Spears & I Pray the Apostles' Creed" as a joke. Then I wrote eight more poems about her. Then ten more. The joke stuck.

Now I'm wondering: why? Our obsessions reveal a great deal about us as both individuals and as a culture, a collective body. And it seems we might be especially enchanted—in the vein of Warhol—of things that both transform and remain the same. See also: Britney on *Star Search*. Britney on *Mickey Mouse Club*. Britney as Catholic school girl. Britney as snake charmer. Virgin Britney. Slutty Britney. Mother Britney. Crazy Britney who has shaved her head and wields an umbrella as the flashbulbs of paparazzi flash all around her. Rehab Britney who becomes Reformed, Upstanding Citizen Britney. She is the thing that both transforms and remains, like every last one of us, but lain out for all the world to see.

Britney Jean Spears was born on December 2, 1981. A Sagittarius, she's extroverted and drawn to the flame of her own fire. I was born on September 19, 1984, a Virgo, drawn to the fire of strong women. We are less than three years apart; we've grown up together.

On September 30, 1998, Jive Records released Britney's "Hit Me Baby One More Time," the song that launched her career. Though it had been originally written for TLC, the song, it is clear in hindsight, was always meant for sixteen-year-old Spears. I was thirteen, enrolled in Mrs. Bough's advanced technology class at Nixa Junior High, a two story stone building next to the Fleischmann's Vinegar Plant. When Marty, my oldest brother, killed himself that year, I learned HTML, built a Britney fansite for my final project, and was one of two students to receive an A.

"What I wanna know," David says to us, "do you guys think her tits are real?" And what I want to do is slap him upside the face for his blasphemy, tell him to leave her the hell alone. I'm sixteen. We are all sixteen here—David, Royce, Jason, Nixon, and I—five unlikely friends, a conglomerate of star basketball players and theater stars. We're in the rec room above Nixon's garage, its deep red walls slathered with golf clubs and Seattle Mariner pennants, framed tickets from the 1996 Chicago Bulls championship and baseball bats. Usually, we're watching sports here and I sit, bored and falsely interested in these things the other boys love, a fact that seems all too cliché now, though true. But tonight I've demanded we watch the MTV Video Music Awards. It's one of the most famous Britney moments: she sings "I'm a Slave 4 U" with an albino boa constrictor dangled around her neck. *Stop looking at her*, I want to tell these boys, *she is not here for you.*

But who is Britney here for? For me? When I pretended to be in love with a woman and the woman broke my heart, it was Britney's "Everytime," her heartbreak song to Justin Timberlake, which became my solace. When I fucked a boy in the sound booth at a rave sophomore year, it was Britney's "Me Against the Music" which pulsed through the speakers, the world a sloppy swirl of glow sticks floating below us. When my friend Jess and I are upset, it is Britney's "Circus" we put on the car stereo, dancing like hormonally charged teenagers as my white Jeep Cherokee scampers down the highway. We do this as though we are sixteen but we are nearly twice that age. I obsess about Britney, as many men like me do, and perhaps, this, too, is part of our gay male culture, a culture David Halperin says revels "in some of its most despised and repudiated features: gay male femininity, diva worship, aestheticism, snobbery, drama, adoration of glamour, caricature of women." It's also about changing and staying the same, like one of Andy Warhol's portraits, like Britney herself, like every living thing.

To me, Britney has been a strange constant. Yes, we've grown up together: unequal acts of returning to a previous self alongside constant transformation.

For now though, it is summer. Paul and I are at a potluck in one of the grand mansions that line Pittsburgh's Fifth Avenue, broken up now into odd, beautiful apartments. We've just argued about Warhol, this city's favorite son, and the women that would consume him—or, like us, he would consume—if he were alive today. Paul is right, I know. Warhol would shake his head at Spears and heave a heavy sigh when he opened *The New York Post*, reading about one of her overwrought scandals.

When Paul and I step outside to smoke, he taps two American Spirits from their bright yellow package. He hands me one, leans in to light it and kisses my cheek, the chaff of his full beard against my stubble. I won't think of Britney then, though we have just talked about her, two men on the happy side of drunk, smoking and kissing and laughing on this porch in Pittsburgh.

ON FAGGOT: AN ETYMOLOGY

AT THE COTTAGE OF ANNE HATHAWAY, which is in the town of Stratford-Upon-Avon, which is in Warwickshire County, which is in the West Midlands, which is in England, which is in the United Kingdom, a portly tour guide points to a fireplace in the kitchen.

"This is where they burned the faggots."

She continues with the tour. "Here is the bed, his second best, which William Shakespeare gave his dear wife Anne. Notice how it is short. In those times, they slept not flat on their backs, but somewhere between upright and reclining. This was out of an old fear: if Lucifer saw one lying flat, he would think one was dead and sweep in during the night to capture the soul." I notice the intricate embroidery, yellow and mint green, on a tapestry down the hall and think to myself, "Jesus, Duane, you're such a faggot."

...

The Oxford English Dictionary lists twenty-six words with fag- as their root, from the late eighteenth century colloquial verb *fag*—"that which causes weariness, hard work, toil, drudgery, fatigue"—to the 1724 Germanic use of *fagotto*, a musical term that implies "with bassoon."

...

At the Pittsburgh International Airport, our flight to London via Newark is canceled. We are shuttled to a nearby Comfort Inn and eat dinner at a dive bar next door. The place smells familiar and a friend turns to me and says, "It smells like a backwater queer bar in here!" Yes! Exactly. Like the first gay bar I went to: Martha's Vineyard on Olive Street in Springfield, Missouri. When I was a heterosexual, I went there one night with coworkers, drank too much, blacked out atop a table, and woke up a homosexual. The next night, I returned newly queer and met a prince—this is when I believed in fairy tales. What is that smell? Cigarettes, spilled vodka, and lube? Maybe. But this isn't a gay bar.

I walk to the bathroom, where beside the urinal someone has drawn a cock on the wall. Above this, someone has sprawled the word *faggott* with two "t"s, which I take to mean, "an overzealous faggot."

...

In his book *Annotations*, John Keene says, "Missouri, being an amalgam of nearly every American region, presents the poet with a particularly useful analogue." I try to understand this, but cannot. From London, I email to ask my mother, deep in the Missouri of both geography and metaphor. She, too, is baffled. One afternoon, as I stroll the cobble-stoned alleys of Soho, the sentiment is all I can think about, though its meaning is still unclear.

...

Three movies terrified me as a child. First, *Return to Oz*. This was 1989 and I was five years old. My sister, age seventeen, brought the VHS home from Aurora Video Source, where she worked on the weekends. In the movie, Dorothy, somehow younger than in the original film and also British, which is why I remember this now, visits an insane asylum. For a year, I could not sleep alone. When I am eight, Uncle Dennis is brought to us, dying of AIDS. The same sister, twenty now, tries to explain and shows me *And the Band Played On*. Among other things, I think the movie is unfair to the Reagan administration and that two men kissing results in death. Which is why, as I watch *Legends of the Fall* in the basement during high school, I am scared for my life when Brad Pitt, shirtless, wades into a rushing creek. I kiss my girlfriend, but think of him.

My favorite *fag-* root in the dictionary is *faggoteer*, "one who makes faggots." British faggoteers: David Bowie, David Beckham, The Spice Girls, Charles Darwin, Julie Andrews, Angela Lansbury, imperialism, Winnie the Pooh, rugby, and parliamentary procedure. Also: Oscar Wilde, Elton John, George Michael, and Harry Potter, though it is unclear whether or not one can be both queer and make further queerness. And yes, Diana, Princess of Wales.

Also worth consideration, American faggoteers: Madonna; Walt Whitman; Calvin Klein; Michael Jordan; Bob Dylan, and more so, his son Jakob; Starbucks; Levi Strauss; Kurt Cobain; and Brad Pitt. Also, Patsy Cline, the cast of *Friends*, and Hillary Clinton.

...

In London, Prince William prepares to marry Kate Middleton. On the television in our hotel room, Andy and I watch oodles of gay men discuss the minutiae of the wedding. In this way, gay men are commodities. *Yes, Alexander McQueen's protégé could be designing Kate's dress. No, the Queen will not upstage the bride. Prince Harry should keep his speech short. Hats are appropriate. White lilies and tulips would be nice. String quartet, not jazz band. Undoubtedly, Princess Diana would not approve.* Oscar Wilde, from the grave: "the highest as the lowest form of criticism is a mode of autobiography." That sounds about right. Wayne says all this "proves that fashion ideas come from fags watching revivals and paying acute attention to fugue and fatigue;" his alliteration is quite lovely. I am a confused commodity, though I begin to understand British queens. And American queens. And that everyone must weigh in.

...

My least favorite fag-rooted word is *fage*, a verb: "the action of coaxing or deceiving; a fiction or deceit."

The Globe Theater is a complete fage. A modern recreation that opened in 1997, the new Globe is believed to be "very similar" to that of Shakespeare's construction, though it is located 754 feet from the original. Our tour guide is an allegory, a tall drink of water on these banks of the Thames. He is married, presumably heterosexual, and at every joke he cracks, I laugh a little too loudly. In this way, I am a cliché, another gay man drawn to an unattainable straight man. It is all language, all syntax. In a hall with posters for Shakespeare's plays, I ask the guide his favorite. He points to *As You Like It* and says "all the world's a stage, and I, just one of its players."

...

At the Bodleian Library, I pick up a reprint of a 1942 pamphlet from the United States War Department: "Instructions for American Servicemen in Britain." Uncle Sam explains "YOU are going to Great Britain as part of an Allied offensive—to meet Hitler and beat him on his own ground. For the time being you will be Britain's guest." What follows is sage advice.

I imagine my Uncle William, my father's oldest brother, fresh out of training. He was likely given this pamphlet. Probably carried it alongside letters from his young wife, my Aunt Marilyn. On page five, as he sailed from the depths of Missouri to New York and on still to London, he likely read, "The British have phrases and colloquialisms of their own that may sound funny to you. You can make just as many boners in their eyes." Did he laugh, as I do now? Or did he, a soldier in the war machine that became the Greatest Generation, take his boners more seriously?

...

In May of 1780, Madame D'Arblay, English playwright and laborious conversationalist, wrote in her diary, "I felt horribly fagged," which means "wearied out, excessively fatigued." In February of 1994, Marvin Willhite, Jr., methamphetamine dealer and my brother, also became fagged.

I will say this exactly one time. My father, my brother Randy, Marvin, and I had lunch at Boxcar BBQ. This is at 1131 North Grant Avenue in Springfield, Missouri. I did not like barbecue, and told them as much, pouting through the entire meal. As we leave, Marvin grabs my arm and says, "Don't be such a little faggot."

I don't say that because it is sad. I say it because it's confusing to me now. Which faggot did he mean? The 1700 use, meaning a person temporarily hired to supply a deficiency at the muster? To bind hand and foot? Any number of bundles—steel rods, wooden sticks, planks? The practice of burning heretics?

I lied. I will say it again. My brother called me faggot in the parking lot and two days later, killed himself. This was with a shotgun in his mouth in the back bedroom of his trailer.

...

My father came back from Vietnam and listened to three songs: "House of the Rising Sun," by The Animals; "Wouldn't it be Nice," from the seminal Beach Boys album *Pet Sounds*; and Buffalo Springfield's "For What It's Worth."

In Bristol, an industrial port city on southern England's western shore, it is a Monday night. Sarah and I go to the Queenshilling, billed as the city's oldest gay bar. For two hours, we wonder if a fellow patron is a man or a woman. Then I hear it coming from the jukebox in the corner: "Stop, children, what's that sound? Everybody look what's going down." My father is a ghost here, as is the bartender and the couple drinking gin, holding each other in a glittery black vinyl booth. I am ghost here.

...

When we visit the ancient Roman bathhouse, I am not interested in the coins, or the curve of stone archways described as "revolutionary." But I do want to understand. What did they wear here? Were the sex acts performed in the open, or in dark corners? How did the bathhouse evolve? My questions go unanswered. In the hot pool below the ten o'clock sun, I dip my hand into the water. A tour guide yells from across the hall, "Stop!" Too much is forbidden, and the rules go unexplained.

Later, in London, I go below the street to use the public restroom. There are five urinals, four of which are full. I pull into the empty parking space. Next to me four men masturbate, tugging their erect, uncircumcised cocks towards the metal pool of toilet. This is like when Wayne says, "I am confused about what's contemporary and what's outdated. I am confused about the spirit of the age." The men glare at me, annoyed that I do not join in. And this is progress: less is forbidden, but the rules still go unexplained.

...

I should be interested in the countryside. At the home of William Wordsworth, I should walk through the gardens and consider the foliage, the abundant daffodils and sizable wisteria bushes that grow along Victorian-era stone fences. But for the last few days, since we've arrived in England, all I can think about is urinals. I take pictures of them at London Heathrow Airport, Shakespeare's birthplace, the Jane Austen Center, sundry pubs and town squares, McDonald's, and now, the visitor center at William Wordsworth's expansive estate, home of the quintessential Romantic poet. Am I romanticizing piss? The places we piss? Is this a fetish? Is this how obsession feels?

...

I have a professor who teaches me to write poems. One day I give him one. He says, "I like this, but make it a little more faggy." I try, but do not know what this means. Later, I add a urinal in the third line of the second stanza to no avail.

...

The underground bathroom we talked about earlier is not a bathhouse; the comparison was not apt, and I need to rectify this.

So in London, I want to visit a bathhouse. I go to Starbucks and research establishments on my iPhone. I decide on the SaunaBar, near the Covent Garden Tube station at 29 Endell Street. Like the underground bathroom, SaunaBar is subterranean, down a flight of stairs below a yogurt shop. I set rules for myself: Do not judge. Do not have sex. Blend in. Face this fear of knowledge.

The fear comes from the aforementioned movie: *And the Band Played On*, where bathhouses are painted as a breeding ground for AIDS. I still become nervous in the locker room, but then I remember Anjelica Huston was in that film before I knew her as a goddess.

The clerk at SaunaBar takes my wallet and cell phone. He hands me a towel and locker key, saying, "Have fun, lil' guy." The rest is mostly uninteresting. There is one attractive man—mid-thirties, blond, slim-but-muscled physique. Let's call him Evan. Evan probably swims a lot. Evan probably has a corporate job in the nearby financial district. How else can this be said? From four feet away, I watch Evan fuck a man. Evan smiles at me, looks for me to cheer him on. I watch. Evan finishes and, interested in the public life versus the private, I follow him to the changing area, where we both dress. From a distance, I follow Evan above ground, onto the street, around the corner, into the arms of his wife and child. I do not know how else to say this.

I duck into a nearby record store and thumb a rare Cyndi Lauper vinyl. Alongside Anjelica Huston, I believe, she is a goddess.

...

Whereas I call them goddesses, my therapist calls the women in my life like Cyndi Lauper and Anjelica Huston escape artists. This man used to be my therapist. I call him a prick.

...

This etymology is a maze. Consider the 1853 term *faggery*, or system of fagging at public schools. Then, *fagging*, the action of the verb *fag*, which probably means "to beat." Another interesting definition, however, is "to cut corn with a sickle and a hooked stick." Jimmy fagged corn, and I don't care, because Jimmy is an Aquarius and too blond for my tastes.

In a tongue-in-cheek sex book I picked up in the bathroom at the Queenschilling in Bristol, we are told, "Fags often suffer from obsessions with men they have never met." Yes; that's the Jimmy we just talked about.

Who is he? Maybe Jimmy Carter or James Dean. Not James Franco, who is not too anything except too perfect.

Somewhere on the internet someone says that *faggot*, when translated from French to English, can mean "meatball." I cannot establish this as fact, but in 1862, Mrs. H. Wood exclaims in a letter to her friend Mrs. Hallib, "Mine is a fagging profession!" Her profession, sadly, is unknown. This was in Romantic-era England. Was she the butcher, the baker, or the candlestick maker? Or was she of noble birth: a duchess, a countess, or a baroness? So much is lost in bad record keeping.

...

I think of fagging professions today: barista, psychoanalyst, and gym teacher. Maybe this is wishful thinking. In the west of England, we spend a day in Bath. I visit Colonna & Smalls Espresso Room at 12a Princes Street, in a small alleyway behind the Royal National Hospital for Rheumatic Diseases. For an hour and a half, I speak with Maxwell, the fourth best barista in the United Kingdom according to the World Barista Championship, a subsidiary of the Specialty Coffee Associations of Europe and America. In an hour, I've thought of all the ways I could move here, date Maxwell, and live happily. Which is to say, hold Maxwell's hand and write him poems. In the next half hour, I've thought of how ridiculous this is. That Maxwell is not even gay. That this obsession has gone far enough.

It is difficult being human sometimes; this living is fagging. In this sense, the action of wearing oneself. Making oneself the fag-end, the last part or remnant of anything, after the best has been used.

A NEED TO KNOW BASIS

MY MOTHER LIKES TO TELL STORIES. She exaggerates truth, if it ever actually exists, and yet, my siblings and I never question the emotional authority of the tales she weaves. They are part, surely as she is part, of our very existence. My mother enjoys the chase of a narrative. And this is a trait I have inherited, most likely one of the very attributes that led me to writing. My father, however, loves facts. Plain and simple.

My father is like *Dragnet's* Sgt. Joe Friday. From 1951 until 1959, Friday, played by Jack Webb, always in gray suit and skinny black tie, introduced every episode with two simple declarative sentences: "My name is Friday. I carry a badge." There is nothing wild here, nothing worth note, really. And yet, the simplicity of the syntax speaks volumes to the man behind the badge. Every week we find Friday investigating a new crime on his beat with the LAPD. Every week he questions a key witness. She is always a woman, and like my mother, perhaps, a person who enjoys the chase of narrative. She posits and interjects tangentially in her own view of the crime. Friday always interrupts and asks for "Just the facts, ma'am." This is not unlike the man from whom I have gained half my DNA. My father, Duane, for whom I am named. My father loves *Dragnet*, which strikes me now as no surprise, the show we watched every week in syndication from our living room in the Ozark Mountains of Missouri.

Since 2005, age twenty-one, I have worn the same eyeglasses: sturdy black plastic frames, standard military issue. Glasses that appear heavy, perhaps, but are not. Glasses first marketed in the 1950s and worn most famously by rock-n-roll pioneer Buddy Holly. The frames I have worn since 2005, hailed as "geek chic" by *Gentleman's Quarterly*, were once my father's. My father first wore these glasses in 1959, the year Buddy Holly died in a plane crash near Mason City, Iowa. My father wanted to be a pilot in the United States Air Force. And though I know little of his childhood on the dairy farm in Dixon, Missouri, my father has told me he loved to sneak away to the cornfields, to lie there, his sight line only corn or wheat, then sky, then planes flying overhead, spraying the crops with pesticides. My father dreamed of becoming a pilot in the United States Air Force.

But my father could not become a pilot because he needed glasses to correct his vision. Instead he dredged through the fields of Laos, Cambodia, Vietnam, and thought of the fields in Missouri, how in all these places the planes fly above him. I imagine my father, with his own astigmatism, squinting to see against the glinting Southeast Asian sun. In 1959, Private First Class Duane Gilson received what the military refers to as Regulation Prescription Glasses, or RPGs, to correct his vision. These are frames made of sturdy black plastic, known for durability and cost-effectiveness. They are called Regulation Prescription Glasses, or RPGs, or Rape Prevention Glasses, or birth control glasses, or BCGs. My meandering here is all, I suppose, an attempt to see what, or perhaps how, my father sees.

A few weeks ago I emailed my father, asking about his deployment in Southeast Asia. Like many soldiers having served in any war, and perhaps the American conflict in Vietnam particularly, he's never spoken at length about this period. Though I assume it was pivotal, and that even this assumption is a gross understatement and overgeneralization. And what, of me, does the fact of emailing betray? Could I not have picked up my cell, dialed the only home telephone number I can ever remember my parents having? Would my father have not picked up, and in the low whistle of his central Missouri drawl, say, "Hell-low?" A question instead of a statement. Could I not have asked, when home visiting just weeks ago, the question already on my mind, without a doubt: for my father to explicate his military career? Over coffee, perhaps? On the back deck? No. I emailed my father because a question of this kind, in a category I cannot even begin to define, makes us both too uncomfortable. Or rather, it makes me uncomfortable, to be clear, to place blame, if that is what it can be called, on me and not my father, sitting on his plaid sofa in the den back in Missouri, a sleeping dog at each of his flanks, a large-print Western novel open upon his lap.

When I emailed my father to ask about Vietnam, I should not have expected elaboration, a narrative of any sort. Instead, via post a week later, I received two handwritten pages, a timeline of his journey in the United States Air Force, which I read from behind the glasses, once his, now mine. I decided to attempt what I already knew impossible: to chase the narrative of my father, or at least, this part of him. I decided to place my word alongside his. What I fear though: there is no map to this place deep inside of him.

...

I enlisted in the Air Force on 10 February 1959. A group of enlistees were sent to the Kansas City Induction Center by bus, where we received our physical examinations and swearing in. We left Kansas City by train for San Antonio: basic training at Lackland Air Force Base.

At the beginning of basic training, every enlistee in the United States Air Force swears, aloud and en masse, an oath. Called "The Airman's Creed," it begins: "I am an American Airman. I am a Warrior. I have answered my Nation's call. I am an American Airman. My mission is to Fly, Fight, and Win." My father wanted to fly, to leave behind the fields of the family farm in Dixon, where he watched the crop dusters fly over, dreaming of his own escape. He was short, 5'6", and perfectly built to be a pilot. At his physical in Kansas City, however, it became apparent he could not see well. On his medical write-up, the doctor likely wrote "not eligible for flight school." Or, "young man, what have you gotten yourself into?"

Dad boarded the train in Kansas City. He rode along that great prairie which sits east of the continental divide, and knew he would never fly.

...

Following basic training, I was transferred across base to attend basic apprentice medical training. We had an opportunity to choose different specialties. I chose veterinary service, and was sent to Gunter Air Force Base in Montgomery for Veterinary Apprentice Training. This was the summer of 1959.

The Air Force Medical Service, or AFMS, became an official entity on July 1, 1949, when the Air Force itself was only two years old. The division was subdivided into six major corps: the Medical Corps, Dental Corps, Nurse Corps, Medical Service Corps, Women's Medical Specialist Corps, and Veterinary Corps. The Air Force Veterinary Corps was always a somewhat vague part of the military industrial complex. During my father's tenure, from 1959 until 1979, their primary responsibilities were animal medicine, treating and rigorously training military dogs; food quality and sanitation, often seen as outside the scope of the Corps, and fodder for both internal and external complaint; general public health initiatives; and animal research. The Vet Corps was small, and my father toward the top of its hierarchy. And I cherish this fact, his position, though the Corps no longer exists, disbanded in 1980 from lack of need and direction.

I have gleaned my father joined the military to escape the strict hand of his own father, a rigid man whom I only remember, and even then only vaguely. My grandfather: spouting racial epitaphs to a busboy at Western Sizzlin, rolling his eyes at my grandmother, beloved by both me and my father, her middle son. I have gleaned my own father longed to learn, and that for the seventh of fourteen children living on a farm in rural, central Missouri, college was not a possibility. The military was a way out. By the mid-'50s, the Korean War was over, and a conflict in Vietnam barely bubbled under the collective American consciousness. My father, to this day, is a quietly peaceful man; that he chose the Vet Corps is of little surprise.

But the map into this part of him becomes blurry.

What is this place even? I fear the country's name: *Place-You-Will-Never-Know.*

...

In December 1970, I departed for assignment to Bien Hoa Air Base, Vietnam.

There is one picture of Dad that I hold dear, possibly more than any other possession. He has traveled to Bien Hoa but is now in a rural village, a haven for children made parentless at the hands of a world political system that regards the process of orphan making as a necessary part of progress. In the photo, my father holds a piglet between his knees. His back is to the camera. A group of Catholic nuns, dressed in shockingly bright white smocks, compose the remainder of the foreground; they watch my farther, and learn how to vaccinate the pig against jungle diseases. In the background, within the doorway of an ordinary building, two children, about eight years old, watch the scene between them and the camera unfold, their eyes wide, their smiles shy, yet obvious.

And though I cannot see the look on his face, I know my father is happy here. Helping, even if the circumstances are shit. Helping, the thing he continues to love today.

...

As I write this, I sit in a coffeeshop in Pittsburgh. I moved here from Missouri two years ago for graduate school, and my father helped me make the move to the western hills of Pennsylvania. Early one sticky August morning, we stood in his garage, in the middle of a little town named Nixa, Missouri. We bickered as we crammed the last of what could conceivably fit into the back of my Jeep Cherokee, two people, both men now, thinking they were experts on packing one's life into a small space. I relented, and let Dad reorganize the trunk. When it came to the two of us on the open interstate, however, I did not relent control of the radio. Though we listened to that which binds us: Johnny Cash, Bob Dylan, Simon & Garfunkel, and Ira Glass in past episodes of *This American Life*.

Twice I have seriously considered joining the armed forces. Once, in my junior year of high school, when I was dead set on attending the United States Naval Academy in Annapolis. Once more, in my senior year of college, when I spoke with a recruiter from the Air Force Officer Corps. "Son, we would love to have you as a writer in our information services division," he said. But our country was fighting two seemingly unending wars under the umbrella of a larger *War on Terror*. "Bullshit," my father told me, "they need soldiers, son. Combat. Don't do this." And I didn't.

Here I am now in a coffeeshop in Pittsburgh. My father's thick black glasses bare fact upon my face. His handwritten timeline lies on the table before me. I pick it up, thumb the script, the place where his hand has brought—*himself?*—to the page. We are all reaching out, and it is, perhaps, the truest cliché. We are all trying, or should be trying, to understand one another.

...

At the end of 1971, I returned stateside, to Keesler Air Force Base in Biloxi, Mississippi.

This sentence, the only explanation after his departure for Vietnam. There is nothing written in-between leaving the United States and returning. Did the war happen, I wonder now? And more so, what is being written through hiding here? Is this self-preservation? In his poem "Vietnam Epic Treatment," Donald Revell goes to a similar line of questioning: "The 20th century? / It was a war / Between peasants on the one side, / Hallucinations on the other."

I remember eighth grade, and Coach West, our history teacher, assigning us a research project. Seven pages on a historical issue from the twentieth century. I chose to write about the American conflict in Vietnam and gave myself over to facts. From 1955 until 1975. Some 58,000 American soldiers killed. Some two million plus dead Vietnamese civilians. Tet Offensive, Anti-Communist Sentiment, Kent State Protests. I am in the eighth grade and cannot understand countless complexities.

I am in the eighth grade and walk into the den, notebook in hand, to speak with my father, "so Walter Cronkite claims we didn't win the war in Vietnam, but I'm finding conflicting information. What happened?" My father looked at me, his eyes widened. It was not anger. It was bewilderment, or some emotion, unnameable, akin to astonishment. "Son," he said, "I can't..." and his voice trailed off. He calmly put down the book in his hands, unfurled from his easy chair, walked to the garage, and locked himself inside.

I don't know if my father was always a quiet man, though I suspect it is so. Statistically, his involvement in Vietnam likely deepened this introversion. Vietnam, the American conflict with the highest rates of post-traumatic stress disorder among its returning veterans. Vietnam, according to the United States Department of Veterans Affairs and explicitly explained in the findings of their "National Vietnam Veterans' Readjustment Study," is also the war with the highest rates of psychological problems and disorders that go unreported, and therefore untreated, amongst veterans from nearly all demographic subcategories, across class and race and any number of indicators. Most-prevalent lifetime disorder, they say: antisocial personality disorder. I will never know if my father is just a quiet man, or if he is quiet with just, external, cause.

But I am trying to write this. I am trying to fill in the holes, to chase the narrative. I am trying to draw the map to that place deep inside of my father, to march through it. Though I fear this place is called *You-Will-Never-Understand*, I do know this: a river leads me there, a steady stream named *You-Must-Never-Stop-Trying*.

ESSAY AFTER MARIE HOWE

YOU SHOULD GO HOME, Will tells me as I hang up my suit in our hotel room. Twelve stories below, the Chicago River begins to thaw; chunks of ice as big as people or cars or small homes float east into Lake Michigan. I have just finished my first academic job interview and ask Will now, *Why does the MLA have to be in January in Chicago, for Christ's sake?* He ignores this. *You should go home.*

My mother lies in a hospital suite at St. John's in Springfield, Missouri, following a stroke. I call American Airlines, book myself on a 6:45 flight, and fly from O'Hare to the Ozarks for one night. She is coherent and tired and frustrated my father can't bring her a decent nail polish. I bring silver specked with tiny black crystals and paint her nails. Sleep beside her bed to give my father a break. The next morning, I fly home to Washington, DC, where I am a PhD student. Following her initial stroke, my mother has another and the doctors induce a coma. In a few days time, they diagnose her with acute lymphocytic leukemia. It is the beginning of the semester and I can't go home again so soon. Or I won't.

I love teaching living poets to undergraduates, many of whom, even at the elite northeastern school where I've somehow ended up getting my doctorate, are surprised to learn there are living poets. One of my favorite poems to give them: Marie Howe's "What the Living Do." Writing to her dead brother, Howe explains: "For weeks now, driving, or dropping a bag of groceries in the street, the bag breaking, // I've been thinking: This is what the living do. And yesterday, hurrying along those / wobbly bricks in the Cambridge sidewalk, spilling my coffee down my wrist and sleeve, // I thought it again, and again later, when buying a hairbrush: This is it."

As my mother sleeps—a euphemism Will gives me when I have trouble sleeping from thinking about my mother—my father slides a mauve vinyl recliner beside her bed. He takes a laptop out of a child's backpack. *If you're going to stay here so long,* my sister told our father, *you can at least play solitaire.* But our father doesn't. He connects to the hospital's Wi-Fi and logs on to our mother's Facebook account.

He starts commenting on pictures. He writes in the voice of his wife, of my mother, comatose three feet away. On a link I post to a writing residency where I've been invited as a faculty member, he says, "Our son has a special spot in mine and his Dad's heart and it's hard to see him so far from us so we are leaving it to his friends to keep him in line and safe." On a picture of my sister's youngest, "Nana sure loves her baby Ella!"

We're shocked. *This is some Grade A fucked-up shit right here,* I tell my sister over the phone. When she asks our father why he's doing this, he shrugs. *It keeps her here with us, I think?* My mother's breathing machine bleeps beside him. She's asleep and he's awake, updating her Facebook. This is what the living do.

LEARNING TO POEM

> A strange den or music room
>   childhood
>   - Frank O'Hara

MY MOTHER WORKS at the Aurora Family Care Center, a low and long brick nursing home on the east side of town, set back from the highway next to a trailer park, shielded from both by two lines of scrubby pine trees. The nursing home is outlined in sidewalks, the sidewalks divided into quadrants by breaks in the concrete. Like this I learn about the square, the rectangle, the line, and loveliest: the rhombus. Every morning, one of the residents marks sections of the sidewalk in chalk and every afternoon I count these. The ones that are marked and the ones that are not. She asks me about simple counting, to produce answers by way of addition and subtraction. She used to be a high school algebra teacher and it is 1989 and George H. W. Bush is president and the San Francisco 49ers just won the Superbowl and Madonna sings "Like a Prayer" which thank god is not "Like a Virgin" and I am five years old, the unexpected son of a nursing director and a government health inspector, counting sections of sidewalk edged in brown and browning crabgrass, wearing acid wash denim jeans cinched at the ankles and waist.

    When your mother is the head nurse, certain privileges are afforded you. I roam freely, areas reserved for staff—kitchen, nurses' station, linen closet—and for residents—dining hall, game room, courtyard. The land here is parched, my father says, and the pine trees, the shrubs, and the ivy in the courtyard show the effects of a spring that never came. A warm winter that, without warning, is now an endless summer. When Orderly takes her smoke breaks in the courtyard, I watch her five minute liturgies from behind a cluster of bushes nearby, the bushes where I bury quarters Diabetic Room 45 gives me to fetch her peppermints from my mother's purse. By July, I will be able to buy the Pink Jubilee 25th Anniversary Barbie at Walmart, the one my father refuses to buy me. The weight of having a son in flux with the weight of being one.

The world outside this building displays every sign of natural, brown death; the inside is all artificial, white life. White walls! White tiles! White florescent! My mother's white shoes and white uniform and how everything on laundry day smells of Clorox! I love the Clorox smell. When I take home the Bush-Hidden Quarters, I lock myself in the bathroom, pull the step stool to the sink and fill it with hot water and bleach, just as I have seen my mother do. I remove the Bush-Hidden Quarters from my Kansas City Chiefs backpack and wash them. My thumb rubs again and again across the face of George Washington. My skin puckers where it rubs the quarters, under the conditions of bleach and steaming water. In my room the Bleach-Clean Quarters gleam in the Kraft Mayonnaise jar where I keep them. The jar I keep hidden in my closet, buried amongst Legos, a baseball bat, and the My Buddy Doll that now wears the sweatshirt I have outgrown, a red hoodie that says *Daddy's #1 All Star*. I will never remember wearing this sweatshirt, though pictures are able to dispel myth into fact. At night, I lie on the floor of my closet and smell the Bleach-Clean Quarters as they pass through my fingers back into their jar, as the sheen of them catches light from the flashlight I have stolen from my brother and brought into the closet. Light catches and refracts in the dark of the closet.

When your mother is the head nurse, certain privileges are afforded you. I am five years old and in those hours where my parents' jobs overlap, I have innumerable surrogates—Line Cook, who makes his tattoo mermaid dance for me in the kitchen just off the dining hall; Diabetic Room 45; *Designing Women*, Dixie Carter, Delta Burke, Annie Potts, and Jean Smart in the TV room; the bushes where I keep Bush-Hidden Quarters; sometimes my sister, when she does not have cheerleading or college prep or boyfriends. My favorite surrogate is Mr. Williams and by proxy, Frank O'Hara.

For most of his life, Mr. Williams has been a drama teacher in New York City and back at our house, I pull the atlas, the one from State Farm Insurance, from my father's bookshelf. This book I am allowed. Unlike the Bible, the one my mother reads to me before bed, where people die and then die and then ride back on a cloud of black fire atop a black horse and then the black book is shut, edged again in gold and put high on a shelf named *No: Do Not Touch*, or *Never*. Unlike the Bible, the atlas is a book of possibility. I open to the State of New York and there above the smallness of Syracuse is a detail of *The City*. I trace the island of it.

It is not just miles that separate *The City* from Aurora, Missouri.

Mr. Williams is here to die. This is a nursing home,

everyone is here to die and sometimes, as is the case with Mr. Williams, the dying does not come steady. Not like a train. More like a raft on a great river of white water, where the floating is lackadaisical for mile after mile and then drops, sometimes without warning, foot after free-falling foot. This is AIDS, which a five year old has no concept of; this is 1989 when few do. Mr. Williams was born near here in his parents' bed, in a home that has long since been razed, or left to self-razing. Mr. Williams has come back to these Ozark Mountains, to the place of his birth, to die.

It is Tuesday, an afternoon in May just before summer. Like most other Tuesdays, I have watched *Designing Women* with Mr. Williams in the common area after school. I walk beside his wheelchair and like this, we travel back to his room—place of innumerable wonders among the doldrums of a Southern nursing home. At the end of the hall is the private suite where Mr. Williams spends his days dying, though I have little concept of this. No way of comprehension. Perhaps this is why he enjoys my company, why he invites me into the bedroom he has filled with prints emblazoned MoMA and Whitney and Guggenheim. With a throw blanket made of African tribal fabric. With a record player and neat, alphabetized rows of vinyl. Our favorite, Ella Fitzgerald. And books. I am most amazed by the books, a vast library spread out before me. Are these forbidden? I know few beyond the atlas and the Bible.

Yet, I know much of possibility and impossibility. I am five years old.

Mr. Williams is going blind. I read aloud to him every afternoon, practice for school sanctioned by both my mother and Mr. Williams. When I stumble to a word I do not know, which is often, Mr. Williams bids me spell the word aloud to him. He teaches me to pronounce it and gives a definition I do not or cannot understand. It is an afternoon just before summer, extra ordinary, the interim that only a balmy Tuesday in May is able to be, in a place by a trailer park and a highway, surrounded by scrubby pines and outlined in gray concrete that seems endless. I pull a book off the shelf, little with an electric orange cover.

It is *Lunch Poems*, by Frank O'Hara.

I am five years old and it is the first book of poetry I encounter. The words in exotic combinations hold innumerable possibility, though I understand neither these combinations nor these possibilities yet. I am five years old and something sparks. Mr. Williams listens as I read aloud to him what Frank O'Hara has written: "Mothers of America / let your kids go to the movies!" I am, unbeknownst, in love with the ghost of a poet, a man who will haunt me, thank god, for the rest of my days among the living, into whatever comes thereafter.

I am thirty years old now and pull a book off the shelf, little, with an electric orange cover. When I walk to catch a bus or to buy a newspaper, I count the squares of sidewalk, adding and subtracting them in my head. I am thirty years old and I live in Washington now, comfortably, though it is not home. I write poems. Now I am queer and can tell you about AIDS. I can give you the definitions to words, which I do not know where—but I do know—I have learned. I am thirty now and listen to Ella Fitzgerald, her hopeful sorrow the metaphor I am still unlocking, all these years later. Clorox is one of my favorite smells. I am thirty and I go to the movies with friends or with boyfriends. Or sometimes I go alone. It is nice to be alone but not alone in the dark. I think of Mr. Williams. I think of my mother, thankful she let me go to the movies.

I am thirty years old and I pull a book off the shelf. It is *Lunch Poems,* by Frank O'Hara.

BOYS ON THE SIDE

I break out of my body this way,
an annoying miracle.
                                    - Anne Sexton

NICK CAME TO FRESHMAN COMPOSITION in a baggy Taco Bell t-shirt and too-short Umbro shorts. He wore this every Tuesday and Thursday, even as fall became winter, when he came to class decidedly less. I gleamed Nick's eyes were brilliantly green and perpetually glossy behind his shaggy bed head. On our first day, Nick explained he came from trailer trash in the wrong suburb of this college town and that his favorite poem—I will never forget this—was Anne Sexton's "Ballad of the Lonely Masturbator." It's a horrible poem, but daring, I suppose, and especially daring for a poor skater boy at a second-tier state school to admit knowing, let alone loving, in a room full of boys from better towns on basketball scholarships.

Fuck slugs and snails and puppy dog tails. Here, a failed thesis: sensitive boys, we are made of our mothers' intuitions. We are all drawn to strong women. Like Nick to Sexton, or Woody Allen to Diane Keaton, or me to Britney Spears, or an infinite number of queers to Diana Ross, Elizabeth Bishop, and Hillary Clinton, we are all drawn to the fire of beautiful, intricate women. Look at the movies we love. We are our mother's boys. *Fried Green Tomatoes, Steel Magnolias, Waiting to Exhale.*

I'm thinking now of 1995's *Boys on the Side*. Scorned Whoopi Goldberg (Jane, dyke), Drew Barrymore (Holly, bubblegum), and Mary-Louise Parker (Robin, AIDS), drive a mini-van from Pittsburgh to Arizona following the accidental murder of Holly's woman-beating, drug-dealing boyfriend. *In a word*, my friend Howard would say, *fabulous*. It's campy and poignant and the perfect movie for gay men. We, I suspect, get it.

Just across the Monongahela River in Pittsburgh where Holly murders her lover in *Boys on the Side*, is the immaculately manicured campus of Chatham University on what was once the estate of Andrew Mellon. Since its founding in 1869, Chatham had been an all women's institution. Following my stint as a graduate assistant at the state school where Nick was my student, I came to Chatham as a teaching fellow working towards an MFA in poetry. On the first day of classes, I faced a room of curious stares from a variety of young women, from inner-city public school graduates to wealthy descendants of the Carnegies; men on this campus, even amongst faculty, are rare. I stood there thinking of another movie, *Mean Girls*. Giving her student a pep talk before the state math competition, Tina Fey turns to Lindsay Lohan: "There's nothing to break your focus, because not one of those Marymount boys is cute." There was nothing here to break my focus. No cute boys were in the room.

In a 1983 issue of *College English*, John Rouse wondered, "Surely there is a seductive element in the relations we have with students, in our effort to help these younger ones enter into new experience, or take it in." To be fair, I was only 22 when Nick was my freshman writing student, and he only 19. He reminded me of—*he very well could have been*—my boyfriend just a few years prior. Nick came to my office hours only once, days before Christmas break. I was surprised when anyone showed up at my office, tucked in the top floor of Pummil Hall with moldy ceiling tiles and stained, dung colored carpet. It was the first time I'd seen Nick in almost three weeks and I was surprised, too, by what he wore. Not the usual slouchy tee and soccer shorts. No, Nick knocked on the door in a white Oxford with sweat stains around the neck, fat corduroy pants a few sizes too big, and his long hair pulled back into a hairband. Nick plopped into the chair across from me, folded his hands atop my desk as if in prayer, and said, *I'm here to talk to you about my grade.* I stared at Nick's temples, wondering if he borrowed the headband from his girlfriend.

At Chatham I was assigned to teach *Fundamentals in Critical Theory*, a joke that begins something like a faggot, thirteen lesbians, and Sigmund Freud walk into a bar. Where my students at the state school had been meek or disinterested, the women at Chatham were Janes, Hollys, and Robins driving mini-vans through the desert and pushing back against every idea I, or the theorists we read, brought to the proverbial table. Here, a bias: Margaret was earnest but appeared meek; she was nondescript, really, with shoulder length brown hair wet from her morning shower and pulled back into a ponytail; she played field hockey for the school, I think, but wasn't a star player; Margaret sat in the third row of desks beside the window, a forgettable geography on the map of any classroom. With equally nondescript expectations, I assigned Margaret to lead discussion on psychoanalytic theory. *Basically,* she began, *Freud was full of bullshit.* She gave a rousing narration of women rejecting the phallus, from Sappho to Toni Morrison, in under ten minutes. I was impressed. More importantly, Margaret was right.

Humor me: straight men ruin most things. They're competitive. Every war in recorded history has sprung from this competitiveness. And I think this violent nature, this drive in straight men to be at the top, alone, is in part what brings women and gay men together. Our mother's children, we are drawn to the films of strong women time and time again. In his book *Working Like a Homosexual*, film scholar Matthew Tinkcom explains, "The link between queer men and female stars occurs through a perception on the part of the queer fan that glamour marks the achievement of becoming through the expense of labor something that he is not allowed—that is, the privilege of representation." Tinkcom goes on to link capital accumulation to vehement patriarchy, which serves no one, of course. But his last point, that gay men watching female stars provides "the privilege of representation" seems perhaps outdated. Gay men are everywhere now on television and silver screen. Yet, we still turn to these women and their movies.

Like me, watching *Boys on the Side* in the living room of my Washington apartment in 2014. Beyond the window, a gay soccer league holds their Saturday afternoon match. But my attention isn't there, on the glistening bodies of men in shorts with sculpted calf muscles. It's on Whoopi and Drew and especially Mary-Louise. I love their world without men. I love that they fight, yes, but espouse loyalty in spades. For much of the second half of the film, Jane and Robin are at odds, scorned lovers of sorts, until Holly gets arrested, taken back to Pittsburgh, and put on trial for the murder of her dead-woman-beating-drug-dealing-baby-daddy. In perhaps the most poignant moment of the film, Robin shows up unexpectedly and confronts Jane on the steps of the courthouse: *All right, this is the situation. I am still angry…Holly is just as much my responsibility as everyone else's, and so are you. Because you are my family and I love you.* At our best moments, gay men can relate to women in this way: we understand the necessity of uniting against patriarchy and the havoc it reeks on our world. We like a mission, a rally, a road trip, *A family*, my friend Will always reminds me, *we choose.*

Forgive me, the poet, for this underwhelming volta: at Chatham, thirteen women and I, in a room without reliable heat or air conditioning but with windows overlooking the east end of Pittsburgh, had hard conversations. I know now, and yes, how petty it seems, that for my part this was because there were no boys around. No one's affection for which I fought. We tried harder. We are all a little bit Whoopi Goldberg, Drew Barrymore, and Mary-Louise Parker, better for pushing boys to the side. We are all our mother's children.

And now that I teach both men and women again, I know to push everyone harder, something I fear boys are still not accustomed to, especially straight ones. When Nick visited my office, I said I hadn't seen him in weeks, but this is a lie. He had not been to class, yes, but I had seen him the week before at a bar downtown, The Outland Ballroom. Had I known Nick was in a band? I think he wrote an essay about this, but I didn't know he'd be strumming bass that night. I had been fighting with my on-again, off-again, currently-very-off boyfriend Cameron. Anna, a fellow graduate assistant who had just broken up with her girlfriend, suggested we drink.

So we did. To excess, out of plastic cups with melting ice and too much cheap vodka that tasted like charcoal. From stage Nick saw us and waved. I waved back and leaned over to Anna, whispering-not-whispering, *Isn't he fucking cute?* Nick was cute. And smart. But also dumb; how hard is it to pass a freshman composition class?

Their set finished, Nick came up to the bar. *Nick, my boy,* I said, knowing I was sloppy, too drunk to be talking to a student, way too drunk to be talking to a student on whom I had a crush. *Yes, Captain?* he asked me, using the nickname my students had taken to calling me under Nick's charge. *I've been thinking about that poem. It's total shit, but there's that quatrain that slays me every time.* I raised my plastic cup. *The boys and girls are one tonight. / They unbutton blouses. They unzip flies.* Vodka and cranberry juice sloshed over my cup's rim, trickling down my arm and dripping onto Nick's shoulder. *They take off shoes. They turn off the light. / The glimmering creatures are full of lies.* Nick, smarter than I'm giving him credit for, got up. *I'll come by your office hours soon, if that's okay.* He left.

I gave Nick an A-. At best, he deserved a low B. Probably a C. He was average. He was average but a cute boy and he got more than he deserved because I was embarrassed. Sexton ends her ballad: *They are eating each other. They are overfed. / At night, alone, I marry the bed.* She's not talking about teaching, but here's what I know now: I wouldn't make the same mistake today. Humor me: boys are overfed. My students deserve to be pushed harder. Something I learned at Chatham, where a faggot, thirteen women, Sigmund Freud, Whoopi, Drew, and Mary-Louise all walked into a bar. We are all our mother's children. Thank god, we are.

DIRTY SOCKS: KE$HA & QUEER THEORY

It *feels* queer, and good.
- Eve Sedgwick

HE SMELLS LIKE FLOUR and yeast and cumin. Like the Ethiopian food we had for dinner. *All the blogs say Dahlak on U Street is the best. / Yes, can we please split the check?* I suggest a change of venue: Omega Bar in a carriage house off P Street. *We can walk from here. / Boys dance in their underwear.* We are boys who never stay out this late. Good boys. But tonight we dance atop a vodka-sticky table and I tell him—*I love this song*! The room hums. *While you're here in my arms, let's make the most of the night like we're gonna die young.* He leans down, his temple to my cheek, and I taste sweat. Which is to say, I taste salt and coriander. And when he kisses me, Ke$ha thrums, *Young hearts out our minds.* We are. Or I am, kissing this married man in Washington. His husband in San Francisco. We kiss and at bar close, share a taxi home. *Kiss me, give me all you've got.*

But try as I might, here, this, him, all of it, is not and will never be home.

To name something is to make it home. To name someone is to give them credence, to allow them into your own body. "A rose by any other name," Juliet tells us, and we see how well that worked out for her. I choose instead a pronoun. He is a visiting writer at the university where I have just begun a PhD. Where I am adrift, in many ways, in what I am doing here, in this city, in these classes, in the shitty apartment I share with Johnny Cakes, the sixty-five-year-old-queen who smokes clove cigarettes outside my bedroom door. We have an alley view and an infestation of bedbugs. So I miss a man named Paul and Pittsburgh, the city where we fell in love at the head of the Ohio River with all that promise of Western Expansion because who knows what's beyond Toledo, St. Louis, Topeka, Salt Lake? We don't, but the thought of it is promising. Washington, however, sits in a swamp nobody else wanted. This is widely known. It is a geography that offers no promise. That demands perseverance. So I meet a boy from Rust-Belted Indiana. His thick-framed glasses fronting sad eyes mirror my own. His hair is blonder, and thinner. He is taller, ten years my senior. Maybe fifteen.

Our first conversation in a stairwell between our offices: Elizabeth Bishop and ghazals. Of how we are both queer and poets and of Midwestern stock. Our second: what a fascinating city we have here. How we are both lonely and queer. Our third: we are queer. Dinner? *How does Ethiopian sound?* Dinner becomes one beer, two, three. The go-go club. Boys on the bar in their underwear. We bare vodka doubles with a splash of seltzer. Four, five, now six. We are sloppy and in the taxi I blackout with enough sense to roll down the window. To lean my head outside to the passing cars of Dupont Circle, then K Street, then Foggy Bottom, time itself *running like we're out of time*. To throw up on the street, not in the taxi. To let my thick black glasses fall to the pavement.

And perhaps we liked each other enough. Or perhaps Ke$ha was right: we were just *looking for some trouble tonight*. Or perhaps we were too caught up in a future that eluded us. I had just broken up with Pittsburgh. With the first man I'd imagined having a family with, a house, a dog, vacations, fights, counseling, reconciliation, mid-life crisis. The whole lot of it. And the other poet, he and his husband were fighting, or not talking, or taking a break. He smelled of gasoline.

Perhaps in that taxi speeding by the most powerful unlit office buildings in the world, we were ready to stop. Lee Edelman says, "What is queerest about us, queerest within us, and queerest despite us is this willingness to insist intransitively—to insist that the future stop here." For an instant I believed Edelman. That night. Through the rest of the semester and Christmas and New Years. Through the reelection and second inauguration of Barack Obama, the most hopeful turned most disappointing president of our time. Through drone attacks and Wikileaks. Through my sister's worsening MS. Through Hurricane Sandy. Through my brother's umpteenth return to rehab. Through the umpteenth Israeli airstrikes on Palestine. Through Obama telling us to not give up hope and Edelman telling us there never is hope. *Fuck*, I remember thinking.

But, like so many things, the year would split into two. Geography evolves. New boundaries draw. Meridians plant. Early that January, I teach Elizabeth Bishop. A vegetarian, I'd long squirmed away from her poem "The Fish," despite its loveliness: "I caught a tremendous fish / and held him beside the boat / half out of water, with my hook / fast in a corner of his mouth." The fish doesn't fight her. He hangs against the hull with "a grunting weight, / battered and venerable / and homely." I am refusing to say that I felt like the fish. But, this is the point of poetry. I felt battered, like a confessional poem.

Which is to say, hooked on my own self-righteousness and reveling in my sadness, *the sadness of an artiste*, in the basement apartment I'd rented with brick walls and perpetually frozen pipes on Capitol Hill. But in reading "The Fish" this time around, despite having read it hundreds of times, I latched onto something I hadn't before: the fish's very queer optimism.

I tire. I tire of Edelman. Of pessimism. Of all that which never comes. But then Bishop writes of the five hooks she saw in the fish's mouth:

> A green line, frayed at the end
> where he broke it, two heavier lines,
> and a fine black thread
> still crimped from the strain and snap
> when it broke and he got away.
> Like medals with their ribbons
> frayed and wavering,
> a five-haired beard of wisdom
> trailing from his aching jaw.

For a poet, it is both wonderful and infuriating when a poem is *right*. Bishop was the fish. Ke$ha is the fish—*Living hard just like we should*. I hate to fucking say it: I am the fish, five hooks scarring my cracked, winter lips. I wear a beard of wisdom. I want to braid it with ribbons until it becomes, as Bishop's oil slick boat does *through* letting the fish go, "rainbow, rainbow, rainbow." We all have a way of doing this, a letting go. I scour the apartment from crown molding to crumb-flecked carpet. Dust and bleach and vacuum. I Windex the windows, compose them into a painting called "Winter Sun." The pipes still freeze. The bricks still let in cold air. But I braid my beard of wisdom, these glittering fishhooks, and put on a pair of thick, green-and-blue-striped socks.

February brings an early spring. A tense shift. My former self—tired of not having a husband—becomes my present self—tired of needing one. Starting with Bishop and moving out, out, out from there—Williams, Komunyakaa, Olds, Howe, Hughes, back to Bishop—I begin to read poetry again. And to write it. I read Michael Snediker on a different way of being queer, one "moored not to an unimaginable future…but to the beneficent crisis of the present." I learn to live in the present, which is also to say: a queer way of having a future. We are always learning this.

Poetry prepares us. Facilitates our own feeling, our own living. Sometimes precedes it. Poets, and especially ones like Bishop, Snediker renders, "show the way one might feel eternal, but also the way one might, more generally, differently, *feel*."

At the same time I read this, I meet another writer, Will. A Renaissance scholar, Will visits my university to give a lecture. It is obvious now: I swoon at lunch. The nautical sweater and maroon corduroy pants. His lime underwear band visible between swift changes in topic: Prince, evangelical Christianity, poetry—*Aww, isn't that cute?*—Britney Spears, *The Good Wife*, gay male reappropriation of animals. Bears and pandas and otters, oh my. *I'm a vegetarian, a recovering binge drinker. / You should be a vegan, a teetotaller.* Cases are made and philosophies shift as ice melts in our overpriced, house-made sodas, hibiscus and passion fruit. Rainbow, rainbow, rainbow.

The happenstance of a spring that comes early and blooms—I do not know how else to say this—in Will's smile. Not all-together shy, but curious. That night, one drink, not seven. Coherent conversation and flirting and a planting of rules. *I have a husband.* But also, a prophecy, throwback to our youths. *Nevertheless, there's something here.* Like a knowledge in the garden we have to till, and prune back, and discover anew.

That night I lose my glasses again. Put them in a rented locker at the bathhouse where we have retired, just Will and me. Through the steam, I watch Will watching me fuck a man that holds no weight in the past my new crush studies, in the present that consumes me, or in the future that presumes us both strangers. Snediker says, "I'm riveted by the idea that joy could be a guarantor of truth—differently put, that joy could be persuasive." For the first time in a long time, I'm as riveted as Rosie, persuaded by joy to let the pessimism of the last year meld into the rough, black stone tiles of the steamroom, blissfully slick with our sweat commingling with the sweat of others. Rainbow refrains rainbow in the soft glow of the dim wattage off this sweat.

But because the present consumes us, Will and I are able to fuck that presumption of us as strangers. *We don't care who's watching when we're tearing it up.* Queer families are chosen this way, in classrooms and coffeeshops. In steamrooms and gardens, queer brothers are born.

In the steam, Will and I steep. Imagine a future where the past pivots in the poems we will write together. In the pages we will collect to make a book. We imagine a future where we realize a new way of being queer. Like brothers, but held dear. Like a couplet that refuses to resolve. *Like it's the last night of our lives...stripping down to dirty socks, music up, getting hot.* A queerness that kisses, giving all it's got. A queerness that imagines a future by needing it. A queerness that builds it. And we keep dancing.

THIS IS NOT A SUICIDE NOTE

MARGOT TENENBAUM, played by Gwyneth Paltrow in what I argue is her best film role thus far, soaks in a gleaming white porcelain tub. A telenova soap projects from the small television perched at her feet, and her mother Etheline, the incomparable Anjelica Huston, worries about Margot, locked in the bathroom, soaking for six hours a day: "Well, I don't think that's very healthy, do you? Nor do I think it's very intelligent to keep an electrical gadget on the edge of the bathtub." Margot looks to her mother from beneath raccoon-ed eyeliner and points to the television: "I tie it to the radiator." *The Royal Tenenbaums* is a film about a family of high-functioning misfits—whose children do things like tie televisions to radiators above bathtubs—and often I daydream of living in their nonsensical and palatial New York brownstone, borrowing Margot's mink coat and sitting on the stoop listening to Paul Simon or The Ramones on a Walkman, or catching falcons on the rooftop.

But I am lying in my own gleaming white porcelain tub. Well, I say my own tub, but this is true only insofar that it is not the same porcelain tub Margot soaks in, but it is also not the tub at my apartment, the one in which I never soak because that bathtub is a dingy, white plastic from which I cannot scrub off the black and green stains, the collective dead skin of myself and those past renters of this Columbia Heights apartment. No, I am soaking in a gleaming white porcelain tub on the other side of northwest DC, in room 226 of the Georgetown Westin. The narrator of *The Royal Tenenbaums* explains about Margot, "She was known for her extreme secrecy." And though I have never considered myself a secretive person, it is in this bathtub, watching this scene on a laptop perched at my feet atop a fluffy, white towel, that recalls to me my secret.

The thing is, I do this sometimes: rent rooms at hotels in the same city where I live because if I am going to kill myself, it cannot be at home. I don't want my roommate to find me and be forced to clean up the mess, or arrange for someone else to clean it up. For my part, I want the clean-up left to someone whose job already entails the bleaching of tub and toilet and sink, the folding of towels, the tucking of sheets. But I don't plan to bleed out, but to ingest too many pills. Or rat poison mixed into a dark & stormy, if it is warm outside, or a Sazerac, if it is not. I will make the mess minimal.

Or, in reality, I will not make the mess. This is why I watch *The Royal Tenebaums*, why I suspect many of us turn to texts—poems, novels, plays, albums, films—as some way of analyzing, or of understanding, or even of caring for, ourselves. Many scholars will belittle this very desire, so central to the likes of Freud and Lacan, but as Leo Bersani contends, "The greatness of psychoanalysis is its attempt to account for our inability to love ourselves and others." I enter melancholy and look to the text, both to dwell within my own melancholy and to look for a way out.

Our conjoined melancholy, Margot Tenenbaum's and mine—perhaps indicative of the relationship white gay men often share with white women—surely emanates from a position of privilege pressed against angst. That I sit in a bougie hotel marking time and seeking out a reflection of myself in a Wes Anderson film made largely by, for, and about white people struggling with depression, undoubtedly speaks to this privilege. But specters of mental illness also unsettle whiteness, as Hamilton Carroll argues that a primary "project of white dominance is to achieve stability." By their very nature, thoughts or acts of suicide circumvent the very idea of white stability. Likewise, Drew Daniel explains how, "The interpretation of melancholy turns upon a basic human question whose pressure persists within the present: What happens when we encounter the emotion of another?" This emotive encounter with others provides a radical potential for thinking how we might coalesce with bodies more deeply entrenched in public violence vis-à-vis the state and its various cultural apparatuses. This encounter may also account for why we read, to begin with, or later, why we study and critique and write.

When asking to speak to a therapist at the University Counseling Center's walk-in clinic, you are handed an iPad. A questionnaire of no less than fifty questions begins by asking: *On a scale of one to five, one being not at all likely, five being very likely, what is the likelihood you will attempt to kill yourself today?* I laugh. I laugh and tap a bubble next to the number two, reasoning that if I were actually going to kill myself today, I would not be at the University Counseling Center, but also that I woke up thinking about it again, so the act is not completely outside the realm of possibility. A hypothesis: people like Margot Tenenbaum and I will not kill ourselves. The cultural mythos of the suicidal writer is strong—from Edgar Allan Poe to Virginia Woolf to

Sylvia Plath to David Foster Wallace, to name just a few disparate examples—but given the number of writers who *haven't* committed suicide, the ones who have off'ed themselves are the exception, not the rule. Those like Margot Tenenbaum and I may saunter through long bouts of melancholy or depression, but we are too vain to actually kill ourselves, as Joan Wickersham, in her memoir *The Suicide Index*, explains: "when you kill yourself, you kill every memory." My brother Marty killed himself nearly two decades ago, and as I recently stood in the frozen foods aisle at Trader Joe's eyeing cartons of pistachio ice cream, Marty's favorite, it struck me that I could not remember his face. This will not do. Vanity arguably killed Narcissus, but there are times it keeps me here among the living.

Onscreen Margot comes across as the most suicidal of the Tenebaums, quite a feat given that within the film's narrative, her brother Richie, played by Luke Wilson, attempts to kill himself in the bathroom as Elliot Smith's "Needle in the Hay" scores the soundtrack. But Margot, like me, like many writer-scholars, is vain. She never appears without her bobbed hair perfectly straightened or freshly polished nails. Rarely without the luscious, full-length mink coat, a signature jacket that rivals any look the real-life living Gwyneth Paltrow might wear. Absolutely the best dialogue from *The Royal Tenebaums* comes in a scene where Margot is standing on the street donning this coat, a suitcase in hand. Her husband, Raleigh Sinclair (Bill Murray) asks, "Do you not love me anymore?" And Margot answers, "I do, kind of." During the saddest parts of my life, this is a motto for daily living, for the "dolor of pad and paper weight," Theodore Roethke might say, or "the blue TVs flashing," as Ted Kooser might put it. "I do, kind of," is the anthem of every person-who-entertains-the-thought-of-suicide-but-will-never-actually-do-it. "I do, kind of," is, queerly perhaps, too, the anthem of many critics when asked why we "love" (or devote so much of our time to) the texts that consume our work.

Marty left a suicide note, and for years I dreamed of what it might say. (Our parents forbid us to read it, and at a certain point demanding, "hey, let me read your oldest son's suicide note," becomes gauche.) Eventually, these dreams stopped. My brother was a high school dropout, and I once read a reconciliatory letter he wrote our mother from prison. The letter was riddled with comma splices, and when I took a class titled *Modern English Grammar & Poetics* in college, I thought of that letter, likened his splices to the caesura of a poem, the complete pause in a metrical line. Pause: when I thought of my brother's suicide note, I dwelled in the House of Grammatical Sanctimony. We, the persons-who-entertain-thoughts-of-suicide-but-will-never-actually-do-it, are, in our melancholic drifts, some of the biggest assholes you will ever meet. In *The Royal Tenenbaums*, Richie (a sexy, drug-riddled Owen Wilson) is a childhood neighbor of the family, a surrogate brother of sorts who admits to Margot's father, "I always wanted to be a Tenenbaum." Richie is a novelist—pulp westerns, mostly—and on the phone with Margot, he asks, "Why would a review make the point of saying someone's 'not' a genius? You think I'm especially 'not' a genius?" Richie is not satisfied with Margot's answer, or refusal to answer, and when he questions her gumption, she answers flatly: "Well, I just don't use that word lightly." We are assholes.

On the banks of the Wabash River in southern Indiana, the poet Marianne Boruch and I sat under a canopy of wilting clematis. She held a poem of mine—which one, I do not remember—tapping her right index finger about halfway down the page. "Huh," she said quietly, "you always do pretty well until the end. Don't lock it up so tight. Leave some room for your reader." In life, an unfortunate pun, suicide is like those endings. Here in Room 226 now, in Washington, DC, not Indiana, near the Potomac, not the Wabash, I'm lying in an all-white bed, watching clips of Margot on YouTube, who sits in a hospital waiting room smoking a cigarette. "How long have you been a smoker?" Ethlene asks her daughter. "Twenty-two years," Margot answers, revealing this one secret, which she has kept since age twelve. She offers no explanation. She withholds an ending. Like the poem should, or like the decision to *not* kill oneself, or like this essay. Or like the text, which welcomes you in, but doesn't tell you where to go.

ELEGY FOR *SKYMALL*

When I look at things, I always see the space they occupy.
                                                    - Andy Warhol

UNDER THE HEADING "Yes, commas DO save lives," are three items—T-shirt, sweatshirt, and 7" x 12" plaque, all in a color described as Chocolate—bearing two lines: *Let's Eat Grandma* and *Let's Eat, Grandma.* This is exactly the type of gift the sister I despise would buy me for Christmas because she knows I would despise it but she could say, "See! It's because you teach English."

I would much prefer the Polaroid Cube (page 106), which pleads, "Life is unpredictable. Record every moment with the newest lifestyle action camera... Designed to take video on-the-go with a recording capacity of up to 90 minutes on a single charge... water resistant, mountable and ready for anything—just like you!" Friends will say I want to make hip, homemade pornos, but in reality I just want to re-enact the shower scene from Alfred Hitchcock's 1960 film *Psycho*. On page 16, a Caucasian baby lies on a Mexican blanket, maracas nested at its feet. Below is a superlative slice of copywriting: "This stand-out baby gift is the whole enchilada. From their sweet rosy cheeks to their delectable little toes, you know your baby looks good enough to eat." For $47.99, you can purchase a tortilla-printed swaddle blanket and matching hat, which turns your baby into a living, breathing Chipotle burrito. I plan on buying two for every expectant family I know.

The majority of the *SkyMall* catalogue is devoted to two types of business travelers. The first wants his home life to closely resemble his business life, a cacophony of airplanes and boardrooms and hotel bars. We are led to believe these men and women are essentially incapable, in need of machines to help them do everything. Glasses that aerate wine, making the hours required for decanting unnecessary. Memory foam neck pillows, which simultaneously massage, play rain sounds, and charge cellphones. The "TreeNanny," which alerts when the Christmas tree needs water by playing a synth version of "Jingle Bells." All of these gadgets remind me of the theorist Noam Chomsky, who warns of our culture's "constant pressure to make people feel that they are helpless, that the only role they can have is to ratify decisions and to consume."

The second type of business traveler is sadder: enraptured by guilt. A large toy section ranges from customizable story books that nestle your child alongside the Disney Princesses or Teenage Mutant Ninja Turtles (perfect for the parent guilty he cannot read a bedtime story to his kid) to the Hushamok Baby Hammock, a finely-tuned oak bassinet ($599.99) that will not only look at home beside your mid-century Eames chair, but also make baby look cool as fuck. Sadder even than these guilt-ridden products, however, are the pages devoted to pets of the *SkyMall* business traveler.

These are dogs and cats and birds (yes, birds) wrought with melancholy over their owner's absence. Here, a platform with sod—*Your Dog's Very Own Yard!*—that drains piss to a basin so pet remains happy and carpets remain dry. Or here, a self-dispensing food bowl that records your voice and beckons your pet to dinner, also spraying your scent into the air, lest the pet suspect the plastic machine with an LED face is not actually you. I imagine the dog lurking away from its bowl disappointed, reciting the end of Jane Kenyon's "The Clearing," where the poet personifies a canine speaking back to its owner: "Do you know— / since you went away / all I can do / is wait for you to come back to me."

In her 1992 novel *The Volcano Lover*, Susan Sontag writes, "There is no such thing as a monogamous collector. Sight is a promiscuous sense. The avid gaze always wants more." I never read Sontag's novels for the reasons I read fiction, for characterization or escape. Rather, I read her novels for their wisdom, their clarity of how we live. I flip through *SkyMall*, knowing every bit of its contents is gauche, but also that I want it all. I want to buy the "museum-quality watch cabinet" that holds 24 watches even though I own only one, rarely worn. I want to buy a map of the United States made from fifty vintage license plates. Or a lamp whose base is the leg of the Wicked Witch; her ruby red slipper's big toe, before Dorothy has stolen the shoes to travel to the Emerald City, serves as a light switch. In January 2015, *SkyMall* filed for Chapter 11 Bankruptcy in U.S. Federal Court, and I fear this is the end of an era—a great loss for American culture writ-large and demise of the truest amalgam available to the poet and cultural critic; *SkyMall*, it seems, might have been, in the lineage of pop consumer artists like Warhol or Frank O'Hara, a metaphor for our collective lives.

(At this point, the essayist usually wishes to say something that draws an even deeper, universal meaning from the catalog of images aforementioned. If you must have it, here: perhaps *SkyMall* represents both the ugliest of American consumerism and our deepest fears of loneliness and guilt, which we soothe by buying things that not only physically surround us, but also coddle us in a Freudian desire to return to the age of curiosity, whimsy, and infancy. But no, the essayist just wants to celebrate *the thing*.

But the essayist would rather you do some work, some digging for metaphors, some comparison-shopping for yourself. Thesis: perhaps *SkyMall* represents the laziness of both essayist and reader.) Scratch that. The essayist just wishes to direct you to erstwhile page 167, containing the Seabreacher boat. Reaching speeds of over 55 m.p.h., the Seabreacher can soar and dive and provide passengers with a 360-degree view of their kingdom from the safety of a vessel customized to look like your favorite sea creature: killer whale, octopus, great white shark.

Maximum occupancy: One.

Price starts at $85,000.

GRATITUDE

Thank you to my dear friends and mentors at both The George Washington University and Chatham University, where I held fellowships allowing me to write the essays here. Specifically, thank you Jennifer Chang, K. Tyler Christensen, Jeffrey Cohen, Holly Dugan, Sherrie Flick, Maia Gil'Adi, Jonathan Hsy, Eileen Joy, Joy Katz, Sarah Leavens, Molly Lewis, Tony López, Justin Mann, Heather McNaugher, Robert McRuer, Faye Moskowitz, Jennifer Murvin, Marc Nieson, Peter Oresick, Tom Mallon, Lisa Page, Douglas Ray, Sheryl St. Germain, Jessica Server, Caroline Tanski, Ayanna Thompson, Gayle Wald, Shannon Wooden, and Sam Yates.

Thank you to Bryan Borland and Seth Pennington for believing in this book, buying me all the pie in Arkansas, and hosting the queerest of pool parties. Thank you to Will Stockton and Howard Anderson for opening their home to me, a writing sanctuary replete with basset hound, mid-nineties Christian rock, and endless supplies of oatmeal. Thank you especially to Will, without whom many of these essays would be complete shit. Finally, thank you to my parents, Beverly and Duane, for pushing me towards the curious, the thing that makes me write.

ACKNOWLEDGMENTS

Thank you to the editors of the following journals and anthologies where some of the essays first appeared:

Avidly—"Britney, Our Lady of Perpetuity"
Folio—"Dirty Socks: Ke$ha & Queer Theory," runner-up for the 2014 essay contest, judged by Paul Lisicky
Fourth River—"On Walking"
The Indiana Review—"On Faggot," which was also listed as a notable essay in *Best American Essays 2014*, edited by John Jeremiah Sullivan
Lambda Literary Review—"Learning to Poem"
Lunch—"This is Not a Suicide Note"
New Delta Review—"Boys on the Side"
Prairie Gold: An Anthology of the American Heartland (Lance M. Sacknoff and Xavier Cavazos, editors)—"A Need to Know Basis"
Queer South (Douglas Ray, editor)—"Riding in Cars with Brothers"
The Threepenny Review—"Michael Jackson & Michel Foucault Walk Into a Bar"
Twelfth House—"Essay After Marie Howe"
The Writing Instructor (special Eve Sedgwick anniversary issue)—"Hey Gurl: Queerness & Romantic Friendship in Poetry"
3QR—"Elegy for *SkyMall*"

THE AUTHOR

D. Gilson is the author of *Crush* (Punctum Books, 2014), with Will Stockton; *Brit Lit* (Sibling Rivalry, 2013); and *Catch & Release* (2012), winner of the Robin Becker Prize. He is a PhD candidate in American literature & cultural studies at The George Washington University, and his work has appeared in *The Indiana Review*, *The Rumpus*, *Threepenny Review*, and as a notable essay in *Best American Essays*.

THE PRESS

Sibling Rivalry Press is an independent press based in Little Rock, Arkansas. Its mission is to publish work that disturbs and enraptures. This book was published in part due to the support of the Sibling Rivalry Press Foundation, a non-profit private foundation dedicated to assisting small presses and small press authors.

CPSIA information can be obtained
at www.ICGtesting.com
Printed in the USA
FFHW01n2047151018
48771158-52867FF